Land of Milk and (no) Money

Roger Evans

Britain's favourite dairy farmer

MERLIN UNWIN BOOKS

Merlin Unwin Books Ltd
Palmers House
Corve Street
Ludlow
Shropshire SY8 1DB
UK

www.merlinunwin.co.uk

The author asserts his moral right to be identified with this work.
ISBN 978 1 913159 52 8
Typeset in 11pt Adobe Garamond Pro by Jo Dovey, Merlin Unwin Books
Printed by TJ Books, Padstow

17 October 2020

You often hear people say that they have put on weight during the pandemic. I know I have. I haven't weighed myself, I can tell from my belt. I used to go to the gym twice a week and I used to wonder if it was doing me any good, it's quite difficult to quantify. But I used to give myself half an hour of stick on the exercise bike and half an hour of hard work on the weights. If you forego that for six months, it is bound to have a detrimental effect. After a life in farming I have two bad knees and they are not as supple as they once were. The gym is open now but I'm not allowed to go because apparently I'm at an 'at risk age'. With a little ingenuity I could exercise at home but that is so boring, I enjoy watching other people in the gym and I keep the exercises going because I suspect that other people there like watching me.

If I have concerns about weight it is the weight of the dog Gomer. To be kind I would describe him as bonny. I have a friend whose teenage daughter was going to her first dance, she came down to give him a twirl and he said she looked bonny and she ran back upstairs in floods of tears!

Gomer hardly has a calorie-controlled diet. For breakfast he has marmite sandwiches. I don't think it is the marmite that puts weight on, rather it is the thick layer of butter between the marmite and the bread. For lunch he either has pork pie or ham sandwiches. After we have had our evening meal he has his big treat of the day, a dried pig's ear. He gets really excited about this. On top of that there is always a dish of dry dog food available. Other dogs come into our kitchen and if they do, Gomer empties the dish. It's not that he wants it, he just doesn't want them to have it. He's a greedy little dog - if he were a seagull he would have that ice cream right out of your hand.

None of this is down to me, I never feed him, in fact I am his personal trainer. His mother is a long-haired Jack Russell and his father is either a Patterdale or Border terrier, I can never remember which, but it is from his father that he gets his thick wiry coat. Earlier this year, in the hot weather, I had him trimmed. The downside of that was that people could see just how fat he was. My eldest grandson has a bum that sticks out a bit and I often comment that you could land a helicopter on there. I don't think you could land a helicopter on Gomer's broad flat back, but you could land a couple of drones. Even the postman is calling him 'Slab'. He spent two days under the kitchen table because everyone was laughing at him.

But help is at hand. Every day I go for a ride in the truck to see if the grass and livestock are growing. This is a very important exercise; I can count the cattle and see if they are all well. One day I counted 70 sheep in one of our silage fields, and we don't have any sheep!

It is during this ride around that I exercise the dog. He gets very excited at the prospect of this drive around although he surely knows what is to come. He jumps into the truck full of good humour. He is always a good-natured little dog; he has always been friendly to people and other dogs. This is rare in a terrier, terriers usually want to pick a fight with everything in the world, and if they can pick a fight with something bigger than them, so much the better. He gets into the back of the truck and then takes up his customary position. He likes to stand on his back legs and between the front seats, he rests his hands on the arm rests, so he gets a good view of where we are going. It also puts him in a good place to lick my left ear and I wish he wouldn't do that.

***

At this time of year there are packs of pheasant poults everywhere and should we come on such a pack on the road, which we often do, he gets very excited. He yelps his excitement, as if to say, 'Just let me out and I'll soon show those pheasants who is boss.' I've got some biggish fields at the top and this is where he takes his exercise. When I stop at the usual place he climbs out in good spirits. He starts out on his exercise, he has all the poise and grace of a concrete block and is about as heavy. He tucks in behind the truck and I don't see him again on our journey unless he should stray from the wheel tracks for his ablutions or if he is distracted by a scent, and then I only see him in my mirrors. Our journey takes us 1½ miles which we do at 10mph, which is as fast as his short fat legs will carry him. He seems to cope ok because he is always close at hand. He likes me, he likes me a lot, which is unusual around here. If I am in the house, and we have a caller, he is all growls, barks and aggression. He looks over his squared-up shoulders, then at me as if to say, 'Look how fierce I am.' He would really like to be a police dog but I can think of several reasons why that will never happen.

24 OCTOBER 2020

We rarely watch *Countryfile* anymore, and when we do, it is only at the end when we want to catch the weather forecast. The last time I watched it there was a Wildlife Trust person in one part of the country telling us what a good thing it would be if there were more field mice about, then we had a Wildlife Trust person in another area promoting the population of pine martins. Never mind that pine martins will eat mice at every opportunity. It is this issue of predation that Wildlife Trusts have never come to terms with. In my own area, they are busy promoting the populations of ground-nesting birds like the curlew and lapwings. But the air is full of red kites, buzzards, carrion crows and ravens. I hope they succeed but you can't have a strong ground nesting bird population and all those winged predators. The two don't mix and never will. Fifty years ago the predators would be in the control of gamekeepers, but they aren't allowed to do that anymore, and it's starting to show.

I remember talking to a retired gamekeeper. At the end of his career he had charge of a grouse moor. On that moor he had grouse and red kites. The RSPB bought the moor next door which was similarly populated. They wrote to him and said 'We know you are killing red kites and we will be watching you.' About three years later he meets the local RSPB fieldsman on the road. The fieldsman tells the keeper that 'when we bought this moor we had grouse and red kites; now we have neither.' What had happened was that the red kites had eaten all the grouse and now there was nothing to eat so they had moved to the keeper's moor. A perfect illustration of the need for balance. It is there for all to see if they hadn't got their heads buried in sand.

Fortunately, we have never had so many programmes on TV about farming. The best is *This Farming Life* which shows caring farmers that work hard and that can only be good for our image.

There's very real life and very real death on a farm. When a vet struggles to replace a prolapsed uterus of a cow, there is blood and the brown stuff everywhere. I have seen quite a few prolapses in my time. In my experience they usually occur in muddy gateways, or if it's inside, next to a drinking trough where it's all mucky and wet. I shall never forget the first one I saw.

When I was a boy, an industrialist bought some land next to our village. First he built a fine house, then he built a model farm and then he bought 12 in-calf heifers. When the first heifer calved she had a prolapse. It was a tight-knit community so by the time the vet got there, there was quite a crowd gathered. Fortunately, the heifer had chosen to calve under a tree, so it was a simple matter to put ropes over a branch and raise her back end off the floor a foot. This meant that the vet had gravity to help him and the uterus was soon back in. I shall never forget the white face of the businessman - this was the first calving he had ever seen. Some of the older boys told him that this was a normal calving but it was rare to have the luxury of a tree to help you! All his heifers were gone in about three days. The fields and farmyard soon looked neglected and after three or four years he sold up and moved back into town.

This also set me thinking about the first year I was farming, I had a little fat Ayrshire cow I had bought. She was trying to calve but the calf was big and I couldn't help her. At about 10 o'clock at night, I phoned the vet. At that time we had three vets, a Scot, an Irishman and a Welshman, and it was the Irishman who came out that night. There was no electricity in the box where the cow was, so he had to examine her by torchlight. This he did and the combination of a big calf and a small cow meant that he decided on a caesarean. He didn't have his caesarean kit with him so he said he would go back to the surgery and fetch it. He was gone a long time, in fact he was gone so long I did wonder if he was coming back.

When he returned he proudly showed me what he had been doing. He had taken the front light off his son's bike and he had fashioned a belt so that he could fix the light to his forehead and perform the operation. You can easily buy such a device now but he was ahead of his time. The operation went smoothly although the calf was dead. The calf was so big we had a job to lift it out, it was so big there is a photo of it somewhere, I don't think I've had a bigger calf since! It was the first caesarean I had ever seen so I was taken aback and I am sure my mouth was open.

The vet gets into his car and gives me some after care instructions. Finally he says, 'For the next five nights, just before you go to bed, it will be a big help if you sprinkle some Holy water on the wound. Do you have some Holy water?' 'No, I don't think we do.' 'Sure, there's plenty in the tap!'

31 October 2020

Pheasant poults go through stages. They are put into their release pen, then they learn to fly out, then they explore their new surroundings, then they go on the road. They move about in groups, there could be twenty in a pack, but there could be 50. I have always thought that their fascination with roads has something to do with their need to eat grit, which is an essential part of their digestion. Should you come on a pack on the road they are often difficult to get through. Not big on road sense, your average pheasant poult. Some will run in front of you until they are so close to the bonnet that they disappear from view, and you don't know where they are. Some will get on to the side of the road but they could easily jump under your wheels. All this time the dog is going berserk, wanting to get out to chase them. Touch wood, I don't think I've ever run one over.

There used to be a man who lived around here that just used to drive through them. I have followed him and he would drive through them fast, he never touched his brakes. He would leave perhaps twenty dead or dying on the road. At least with shooting, the bird has a chance and if they are wounded they are sought-out and despatched humanely.

***

Early evening usually follows the same pattern in our house. My wife, Ann, is sitting on the settee doing a crossword. Also on the settee is the dog Gomer. This is his preferred position in life. He is asleep and he always sleeps on his back with all his bits and pieces on show. I read somewhere that dogs will sleep 80% of their time, I suspect that this is an average figure, I think that Gomer is a mid-90% dog. He has one eye open. I can't decide if his eyelid comes open because he is lying on his back or if he is watching me. I am sitting in my usual armchair, on my knee is our daily paper and the TV is on.

There is nothing interesting on, so I decide to wind things up a bit. I adopt a sort of gaze, I'm not looking at the paper and I'm not looking at the television, I'm sort of looking out of the window, but it's dark outside. I don't have to wait long, 'What are you thinking about?' says Ann. 'I was thinking about getting another dog'. We then get a range of comments that vary from, 'I don't want two dogs in this house,' to, 'you'll never get another dog as nice as Gomer.' We conclude with 'Why do you want another dog?' 'I thought that if we both succumbed to the virus, Gomer would be an orphan, so I thought it would be nice for him to have a brother or sister'. I am not sure about the technicalities of what I have just said but the word 'orphan' is an emotive one and I can tell she is thinking about it. After about five minutes I get 'If you had another dog, what would you get?' I don't hesitate, 'An Irish Wolf Hound.' There is a minor explosion behind the crossword. I don't actually want an Irish Wolf Hound, but negotiations have to start somewhere.

We have had experience of Irish Wolf Hounds in this house. My brother used to have one and he used to bring it here. It was a bit like having a hyperactive Shetland pony in the house. It was huge. I remember on one occasion I just stopped it stealing a freshly-roasted chicken off the top of the Rayburn. The scary thing was that it was so big it had to bend its neck down in order to try and pick the chicken up. My brother used to take it for walks in the woods near where he lives. He used to walk along the narrow paths and the dog would wander about exploring the delightful world of smells that a dog enjoys. And then it would realise it had been left behind and race to catch him up. It would often crash into my brother knocking him to the ground. In fact it was a very real prospect that it would break his legs.

So I don't want an Irish Wolf Hound but I have been toying with the idea of having another dog. We get a lot of pleasure out of having one dog but I'm not kidding myself that two dogs would mean twice as much pleasure. Firstly it would have to be a rescue dog and secondly it would have to be about the same age as Gomer. I have a feeling that somewhere there is a corgi that wants rescuing. Meanwhile I think that the world of dogs is heading for trouble. Puppies are at crazy prices and when you get crazy prices of anything, it attracts the wrong sort of people. That is why the import of puppies from Eastern Europe is such a problem. They say that high puppy prices are driven by the need to have companionship during the pandemic. I can identify with that. Delightful though a new puppy may be, they are not puppies for long and I worry that dog charities will be overrun with unwanted dogs in two or three years' time. It might be ok to watch a new puppy chew the corner of a cushion but less so if a three-year-old bored dog on its own all day, destroys a settee.

7 November 2020

November I have found, is the most difficult time of year to manage dairy cows. As far as I am concerned the best place for a cow is out at grass. I know that there are a lot of big herds where the cows are kept in all year round but that would never do for me. But even my cows come inside for the winter, and the difficulty is to decide just when winter has started. Cows don't mind being cold but they don't like to be wet and cold, who does? Then if it is too wet, they damage the fields for next year and that would never do. So you have to balance all these factors and make a decision.

Ideally, we would like to keep our cows outside until November. What we usually do is keep them in at night at first and then there will arrive a wet, cold day and we just won't open the gates, and winter will have arrived. We are more flexible than we used to be. Years ago our cows used to be either in or out. Now they may be in but if, for example, we get a dry week in

December or January and conditions allow it, we will let them out for three or four hours during the day. They love it, they can have a good scratch on the trees or a nice stretch and they lie on the turf and it gets them off the concrete.

*****

It has always been an advantage to live in a quiet, beautiful area but there was an added plus when the lockdown started. On an average I would only see five or six people a day, (including family), and those five or six would only see a similar amount of people who lived similarly isolated lives. All that changed when lockdown restrictions eased: I have never ever seen so many holiday-makers in the area. Now that the feared second wave is fast becoming a reality I hope things will quieten down.

I only go to the pub once a week now. Fair play to them, they have tried to stick to the rules: if you want to go you have to phone to book a seat and there is no standing at the bar. There is a camping field behind the pub and since lockdown finished it has been full at weekends. There are three areas within the pub and because seats are all designated they tend to sit all the locals in one bar and people from 'off' elsewhere. Because you have got to book a seat and because there are only allowed six at a table, there is often a need to move the seats about. We were a seat short on our table one Saturday and the only spare seat to be found was a big bar stool. This was used, but it put the head of the person sitting on it about two feet above everyone else, there was something of the meerkat about the one who sat there. I was searching for something funny to say, to this effect, but I was beaten to it. 'He looks like a lifeguard on the beach.' And he did.

A reader sent me this story. One day he is taking his dog for a walk over some fields, when he catches up with a lady who is similarly occupied. Her progress has been thwarted because there are sheep in the next field and there were not any sheep there yesterday. My correspondent tries to explain that this is what fields are for, keeping livestock, and the farmer is perfectly entitled to put his sheep in there. But he is wasting his time explaining, the lady will have none of it. She is convinced that the farmer put the sheep there just to be awkward, and he had no right to do so. Probably with a twinkle in his eye, my reader asks the lady something else. Has she noticed that this particular farmer also puts all his gates in muddy places, just to be awkward? The lady is intrigued, no she hadn't noticed that but now she can see that it is true. I expect that she returned home and reported to anyone who would listen 'You'll never believe what that farmer has done.'

I have a good friend who always had this fierce dog with him. If you asked him the breed, he always said it was a greyhound cross. You could see that but I think that if you dug into its DNA you wouldn't have to dig far to find a pit bull, because you could see that as well. Most people, if they want a crossed dog, seek out a poodle cross but there you go. I've not seen the dog for a couple of years so I ask him where it is. He tells me that it is nearly 17 now and spends most of its day stretched out on the settee. In its prime it was quite some dog, all muscle, teeth and attitude, like a great white shark on a lead. It was often asleep under a table in the pub and you had to take care just where you put your ankles. The owner has a young family now so I ask him how it gets on with his children. He says just fine, and then adds 'It only bites one a week.' Of course he was joking, I think we he was joking!

14 November 2020

You will have gathered by now that rugby has always been a big part of my life. At my club during covid there have been 'touch' rugby matches and that is all we are allowed to play at our level.

The hope is that a few people will watch, thus stimulating some interest and income. This sort of rugby is not for me. Rugby is a hard physical game and that is how it should be played. There is plenty of rugby on TV, I particularly like watching Bristol and Exeter because they have come from nowhere to challenge at the very top. I record lots of matches but if the game should prove to be one-sided, I don't watch it. I get no pleasure from seeing someone put 50 points on someone else, I much prefer a 3-0 margin if the game is hard fought, especially if there is a bit of needle in it. But I do have a problem, I write for a sort of newsletter for my club every month and it is not easy to do it when everything is in limbo. I have had to resort to telling (hopefully) amusing anecdotes. If you want to tell people to come to the AGM you have to include content that will hopefully entertain them as well. I have just told them this story, so I will share it with you. They hold a carnival in our local town every year and a few years ago they used to have an event each night in the week preceding the actual carnival Sunday. I remember that they used to have a tractor pull where each pub in the town - there were seven at the time - had to enter a team that would pull a tractor 200 yards on the main street. This only lasted about three years. It was found or suspected that the supposedly neutral farmer who had lent and was to steer the tractor had been putting his foot on the brake if he didn't like the beer in a particular pub. That was a shame because there used to be about 300 spectators.

On the Wednesday evening there used to be a pram race. Teams of three, all wearing fancy dress, had to have a pram or pushchair. One person sat in the pram and the other two had to push him or her from pub to pub just as fast as they could. At each pub the passenger had to rush in and drink half a pint as quickly as they could then return to their pram and rush off to the next pub. There was a dance at the local hall which was the finishing line, so all the teams ended up at the dance.

One year my son and I and another friend we used to play rugby with, decided to enter the pram race but we determined to do it a bit differently. We hired quite good gorilla suits, which made us anonymous. There were 15 teams entered that year and all the entrants lined up opposite the first pub with their prams at the opposite kerb. At the start signal all the teams rushed across the road, the drinker entered the pub and drank the half pint of beer while the pushers waited outside, pram at the ready. In no time at all they were all gone to the next pub. The three gorillas hadn't moved, which raised a few eyebrows. When the last pram had gone the three gorillas strolled nonchalantly over the road, entered the pub and all three sat down and enjoyed a leisurely pint. All in our own time we then went to the next pub where all three of us had another pint. It was some time until people worked out what we were doing. At the dance, the MC started to report on our progress. 'The three gorillas have just left the Six Bells and are making their way to the Boars Head.' Loud cheers, apparently. 'The three gorillas have left the Boars Head and are going back to the Six Bells!' This was true - good pint in the Bells. Eventually we got to the dance where we received a standing ovation. The winning pram had done the course in about 12 minutes, we took 3½ hours! We didn't win obviously, but everyone was talking about us and we had the loudest cheer.

We did something similar the following year. We were a different three, my son and I and someone else. We didn't hire costumes but we dressed up to imitate a local character, a farmer from outside the town. Everyone knew him. He always wore a tweed cap, a tweed jacket, cord trousers and hob nail boots. He always had a pipe clamped in the corner of his mouth. My son and I borrowed or begged our outfits. We did not have to worry that the third member would dress the same, because he was that local character! Annoyingly, he never mentioned the fact that we were dressed like him, not once. We made a similarly liquid journey to the previous year, in fact even more so. But it was not the talking point it had been. You can only do something new once. The most memorable event that year was that I fell down in a pub after we finished and broke my collar bone. Can't think how that happened?

21 November 2020

Nothing heralds the onset of winter so much as when I order my first load of sand. Our cows lie in what we call cubicles and we put a layer of sand in there, so the cows have somewhere clean and comfortable to lie. You could use all sorts of different bedding, like straw or sawdust, but sand has an advantage. It is an inert material, so bugs don't proliferate in it. It is important to keep cows clean, you won't get clean milk out of a dirty cow. Cubicles are designed so that when a cow lies down, should she poo, the poo does not get into her bed but goes onto the concrete passageway. I have never been sure about calling them cubicles. Cubicles as a word, is too near to cow crates (which have been banned in this country for twenty years) and could imply, to those who don't know what cubicles are, a degree of restriction which is totally untrue. In Canada they call them 'free stalls' which is a better name for exactly the same thing.

But it's not winter or cow comfort that I think of when I order that first load of sand. I think of the last corgi we had. She was run over. She was tiny, even for a corgi, she was easily the smallest animal on the farm and because of that I think she had an inferiority complex. We buy big loads of sand, over twenty tons at a time. She liked to stand on the very top of this heap. She liked it so much that she would be on the top before the lorry had finished tipping. She would stay there all day and would bark at anything that came past, be it a human, a tractor or another dog. As we used the sand, the heap would get smaller and she would abandon her position when the heap was three-quarter used and she would then slink off back to the kitchen. But she always seemed to know when a new load was due and she would be waiting for it to arrive. To be fair, we all like to spend some of our time on the high ground and to bark at the world.

There was a double page spread in our local paper that told the story of a corgi on a farm that assisted with moving sheep. As if this were something remarkable! Corgis were originally used to move livestock, they were known as Welsh Heeling dogs, they could nip at the heels of cattle and should those cattle lash out with a kick in reply, the kick would go over the corgis head because of their short stature.

There was a time when we had three corgis living in our house, (corgis have long moved out of our price range, Gomer was given to us free, that's our price range), and the highlight of those corgis' day was to get the cows in for milking. When I arrived in the kitchen in the morning they would make such a clamour to get out of the door, I had difficulty getting the door open. In the summer months they would be off down the fields to fetch the cows and by the time I had a cup of tea, the cows would be well on their way home. In the winter they would rouse the cows from their slumbers in the sheds and have them in the yard, waiting to be milked.

There was a time, when I first started farming, when it was not so common for farmers to own their own 4x4 and livestock trailers. Stock was often taken to market by local hauliers. Our local haulier used to send two or three lorries to our local 'big' market. These lorries would go out in the local area to collect stock from farms and then they would meet somewhere on a farm and redistribute the livestock. All the cattle on one lorry, all the sheep on another. It saved them a lot of time when they got to market because they would only have to enter one queue. It didn't bother me, live and let live has always been my motto. So if I had stock to go to market I wasn't too worried if two or three lorries turned up on our yard. Then I noticed that the lorries turned up on days that I didn't have stock to go. One day, when we were busy, we couldn't get tractors through the yard because it was full of lorries. I asked one of the drivers, why do you always use our yard?'

He explained that it was because of our corgi dog. 'When the cattle have been on a lorry for say half an hour and then let off, they are usually reluctant to get onto another lorry, but your corgi will soon get them on, he will put ten big cattle back on the lorry very quickly, saves us a lot of time.' That's the upside. We had this corgi called Sammy, he was a nasty little dog. We gave him away in the end, our son was only a toddler and we were frightened he would get bitten in the face.

***

It is that time of year again, it's time to open negotiations for our Christmas turkey. Here goes. 'As I don't know what restrictions will be in place at Christmas, I only want half a turkey this year.' He always has an answer. 'We were only going to let you have half a turkey this year anyway.' I do not think it will come to that but if does, I would prefer the front half.

28 November 2020

My brother likes it when I mention him. This is ironic because he never buys my books; he likes his friends to tell him he has a mention. He is a bit younger than me, and we went to the same grammar school but not at the same time. He always maintains that he was caned in his first week at school. He says that the headmaster caned him in case he turned out anything like me.

***

We have had a spaniel bitch to stay for a month whilst its owner was in hospital. It wasn't any old spaniel either, it was a Clumber, which are a chunkier, king-size sort of spaniel. Gomer fell head over heels in love with her and is inconsolable now she is gone. When I go to bed, he is asleep on the settee but sometime in the early hours he sneaks upstairs to sleep next to me on the carpet in my bedroom. I never thought I would say this but I enjoy him being there. He sleeps as close as he can get to my head but he can't get onto the bed, it's too high. I could easily stop him by shutting the doors properly, but if it gives him comfort, what does it matter? He talks in his sleep. No, I am not going to tell you what he says.

***

I recently saw a television programme about a sort of farm, which sounds derogatory, but it is meant to be. There is no chance of making a living by what goes on there, unless there is another income which drives it all. Which in this case there is. But anyway, a cow had calved and the cow had hidden the calf. I have come across this phenomenon lots of times over the years. It never ceases to amaze me just how well hidden those calves can be. We prefer to calve our cows outside if we can, it's so much healthier, but after about 24 hours cow and calf need moving nearer the milking parlour. You can find the cow easily enough, now where is the calf? You know it is there because you checked on it yesterday, but that doesn't mean that you can find it easily now. The calf will be lying down somewhere flattened to the ground. It is amazing just how they can hide behind the smallest clump of thistles or nettles. You almost have to step on them to find them. It is an instinct thing, common to herbivores, who have two main defences against predators: hide or flight, and until the animal is old enough to flee, it has an instinct to hide. The calf we are concerned with today was about thirty hours old, it had been born out in our orchard one weekend and after 24 hours had been moved, with its mother, to the shed where we keep calves with their mothers until they are about a week old.

The routine in the summer is always the same. The cow goes through the milking parlour once a day, to make sure she is not carrying too much milk, she spends her day out at grass with the herd but she spends the night in the shed with the calf so she can feed it and care for it. We had a man working here then and it was his job, after afternoon milking, to return the newly-calved cows to the shed where their calves were. I think there were three cows and their calves at the time and he reported that a calf was missing.

There is a feed barrier down one side of the shed, this is designed for adult cattle and it was decided that it was conceivable that the calf had popped out through the food barrier and would return to its mother sometimes during the night. It wasn't there next morning so after this man had done his chores, he went looking for it. Just to put some sort of perspective on this, it was a beef cross bull calf worth over £200.

He looked all morning and in the afternoon for two hours, to no avail. He went looking again on the Wednesday. I told him he was wasting his time. It was June and grass, cereals, nettles and docks were all flourishing, so the chances of finding a calf that didn't want to be found were remote. There is an old track that goes through our yard, it goes to the next village, and I know he went a mile down that. I didn't want him to go looking but he could be as stubborn as me and he went anyway.

He was just about to set off on his search on the Friday morning. I was getting a bit tetchy by now, not like me at all, as far as I was concerned he had wasted three days already. A Land Rover came up the yard. It belongs to a very good friend of mine, he is a beef farmer and lives about three miles away. After we have talked about the weather and other serious farming matters, he gets to the reason for his visit. 'We had a cow, a beef cow single suckler who had to have a caesarean on Monday morning, the calf was dead and we were desperate to put a calf on her. I came over here but there was no one about. There was a good Limousin bull calf in the shed so I took that, hope you don't mind.' I didn't mind at all; he often buys calves off us in similar circumstances. Just wish he had told me.

5 December 2020

Out of all our family, the one who does the highest mileage motoring is my wife. Just as soon as she has had her breakfast she is off. She is off so often that I have difficulty recognising her when she returns. I think that she should wear one of those identify lanyards around her neck, one with all her details and her photograph. But I will let someone else tell her that. She had a big birthday earlier this year so I changed her car for her. This 'new' car is three or four years old but is the newest on our farm, our family has never wanted new cars. My son refused to buy a really good ten-year-old 4x4 once because it had black alloy wheels and he was worried it was too flash and people would think he was dealing drugs. Have you ever noticed that the families with real, old money rarely buy pretentious new cars? Fair play to my wife, she does the school run for my daughter in the afternoons. My daughter works in the NHS and my son-in-law does not have full time help on his farm.

Last week she pulled into a municipal car park, next to a supermarket, I think they call there for chocolate and other edible goodies. She is just parking up when the gearbox seizes up and the car would move. She gets a local garage to look, but they say it is a big job. She phones the garage where we bought it and they say they will fetch it. She leaves a note on the dash to say what has happened and gets a lift home. Two days later she gets a parking ticket. Seems they believe her story but their problem is that she didn't leave the car within the parking lines. What was she supposed to do, pick it up and carry it and put it in the right place? The car park was only quarter full anyway.

***

In the farming periodical that I take every week, they always print an old farming photo that has been sent in by a reader. Last week they printed a photograph of a group of ladies that were a potato picking gang. The photograph was taken in the 1950s. I just love these old farming photographs. It shows a way of life that people rarely have today. I have got a book of old farming photographs somewhere, but like a lot of things in my life, I can't find it. There is one photo that shows about six or eight teams of horses drawn up at the top of a big field they have been working. The horses have their nose bags on, having a break, and sitting in a row against the hedge are the men who worked them, also having their break. It must have been hard work walking behind those horses all day, no need to go the gym.

***

I am not sure if you are allowed to call them ladies anymore but I will. If in doubt, stick to what you know. When I was younger, before I was married, I was looking after a herd of cows just outside Cardiff. We always grew a field of potatoes on this farm and those spuds were sold on milk rounds. There was a small lorry on this farm and it was sometimes my job to drive it into Cardiff to collect a gang of ladies to pick potatoes. The ladies used to bring their pre-school children with them and the first time I went, I was surprised just how many prams they brought as well. Not push chairs, big old-fashioned prams. Some ladies had children three or four years of age but they still brought a pram. I did not say anything because I was only about 21 or 22 and if your job was to look after the needs of a gang of ladies and you were male, it was best to keep your head down. When we got to the potato field, I used to lift the children and the prams down, all the while trying to be as inconspicuous as I could.

We had to get the pickers home for when their older children returned from school. The first time I took them home I was amazed at how heavy the prams were. It was a struggle to lift them back on the lorry. Some of the ladies had to help me. The reason the prams were so heavy was that they were full of potatoes, they were so full that the children could hardly get in, in fact if there was a child perched on top, it took two of you to lift it in the interests of health and safety, let alone the weight. Everyone knew what was going on but no one mentioned it. The boss knew because he used to take them home sometimes. I am sure he used to factor this in when he worked out their wages.

12 December 2020

This time of year is a lot like when its Wimbledon. I get very little say in what we watch on television. It's the time of year for *Strictly Come Dancing* followed by *I'm a Celebrity, get me out of here.* Last night I was told that I could watch whatever I liked until they came on. Big deal. It was Sunday night, and that is how I came to watch *Country File.* I have the Sunday papers close at hand but I save them for when those other two programmes come on. I have not watched *Country File* lately, by choice, but some of last night's content was a disgrace. What was really naughty was the piece about saving hedges. They quoted the figure of just how many hedgerows had been lost but that figure referred back to the Second World War.

I am not very familiar with the laws regarding hedges, but I have been farming over fifty years and have never taken a hedge out. I would guess that there have been more hedgerows planted in the last twenty years than have ever been removed. *Country File* gave the impression that their removal was ongoing, and I am sure that you need planning permission to remove a hedge. *Country File* showed a bulldozer removing a hedge but the only film they could find was a black and white one, they could not find anything modern. That film in itself was clear evidence that their story was biased.

I've got several big fields where many years ago the previous tenant removed hedges but I am in active discussions with my landlord to put these hedges back in. There is a field map on this table that is about 150 years old, this map shows all the old fields and the field names and we will use this as out blueprint. If *Country File* told this story, it would ruin their narrative. I am not saying that they are lying, but their failure to present a balanced picture so that they can pursue their own agenda, comes very close to it.

***

We were talking about shooting the other day, or rather the lack of it during lockdown. If you take a local shooting syndicate for example, some of the members come a long way to the shoot, so they might meet at a local pub for breakfast. Then, in late afternoon they might return to that pub for a meal and to warm up. Then there would be tips and wages for the beaters, it is not inconceivable that the guns, the people doing the shooting, would put £1,000 into the local economy that day. That sort of money has a cumulative effect. Whatever your views on shooting that is a big lump of money that's now gone. That figure might apply to five or six other shoots that same week in the same locality.

I used to do a fair bit of shooting. We had a family shoot, we used to shoot that about three times a year. It was not very formal, we didn't have beaters, we used to take turns to do that ourselves. Looking back on it now, I used to get most of my pleasure from working my dog. There was a sequence to it all. Firstly, your dog had to find the game and if your dog hunted too far in front of you, the game it flushed would be out of range before you saw it, so having a dog that you could control was a big plus. Then came the most difficult part of the sequence, you were supposed to shoot it - not always successful, this bit. Then if you did shoot it, your dog had to find it; it might be over a river or in some briars, and bring it back to you. If you did all this successfully two or three times on one day, then the dog had been a good one.

So a group of us who used to play rugby together, took a small shoot and that provided a lot of fun, more to do with how we enjoyed each other's company as anything else. At no time on either shoot did we get big numbers of birds. Forty was about the norm and by the time they had been shared out amongst friends and family, I expect that they were all eaten, which is an important principle. We used to hand out birds in their feathers and I did wonder if some of the birds ever got feathered and eaten, or did they end up in a dustbin somewhere. Most shoots around here hand out a brace of oven ready birds which is a much better idea.

Our highlight used to be our shoot dinner when we used to hand out awards. At that time I had a character of a spaniel called Bullet, and he always won dog of the year.

But news comes in of a big estate that has let two consecutive 1,200 birds days. This means that the eight guns will shoot an average of 300 birds each over two days. Why would you feel the need to shoot 300 birds? The idea of shooting is distasteful to a lot of people and this kind of excess is indefensible and only fuels the antis. The cost would be astronomical, 2,400 birds at over £40 a bird, divided by the eight guns, well you can work it out. It has something of a monumental folly about it. People used to erect buildings, mostly towers, they had no purpose except to tell the world that, 'this building has no purpose, but I have built it to tell everyone that I can afford it.' I think that one day, not far away, all shooting will be banned. It will be the fault of big commercial shooting. Small, sensible shoots will pay the same price.

***

Things have been very quiet on the hare courser front this autumn, in fact, now that the fields are wet, I thought that we were going to get away without a visit. All that changed last Friday night. They came and played hell. Gates were thrown off, boundary fences were cut, electric fences were left down. My own heifers got onto the road and were found a mile away. My neighbour had a row of fields that adjoin a council road and he had put locks and chains on every gate. These were all cut off, suggesting that the coursers had some sort of motorised hacksaw. I have been saying for a long time that these people are beyond the law. The law doesn't come anywhere near to solving this problem. The gang were caught a few miles away, so what happened? Well their 4x4 was taken away and crushed. This is standard procedure on all police programmes I watch where a vehicle does not have insurance or road tax, two items which would never cross a hare courser's mind. But they were given another charge. They had travelled out of Wales and had broken a covid rule. I bet that had them quaking in their boots.

***

There is one good thing that comes from the lockdown. If I go to the cashpoint I put the notes in my wallet. And when I look again in two or three weeks time, those notes are still there. They are, if you stretch your imagination, symbolic of what is going on in society. Because if I am not spending any money, neither is anyone else. For some reason it reminds me of when I travelled by train a lot. I used to go to London quite often in relation to the dairy industry, twice a month is often, and I used to use early trains that were used a lot by commuters. I used to watch their behaviour with fascination. I used to recognise some commuters by sight, which means they must have been familiar with one another too. But they rarely spoke to each other, which I found really strange. But stranger still, almost to a man (or woman), each person would be clutching in front of them, like some sort of trophy, a drink of coffee of a famous brand, which they had obviously bought on the station. There were very few exceptions to this, a few eco warriors, that were clutching bottles of water. I ask you, who would want to drink cold water on a dark cold morning in winter? The answer is very few, because I noticed that the bottles of water were rarely used. My point is this. Most of that early morning coffee trade has disappeared in the pandemic, and so probably, have the people who used to make it. There's no end to the financial costs of this present scourge, even the most simple things like an early morning coffee have taken a hit.

Most people are not like me. I do not do any shopping so my money from the cashpoint used to go to the pub or grandchildren's birthdays. My grandsons, on the other hand, are prolific online shoppers; we get white vans here on the farm several times a day. Their parcels accumulate on our kitchen table, I can't believe the amount of packaging involved. There was a parcel here last week, it was about two foot by a foot. I was wondering just what was in there. When it was ripped open all it contained was a plastic rugby kicking tee, about as big as the mug I am drinking out of now.

But the lack of in-person shopping doesn't stop there. All those people who had bought a drink on the way to work would probably go out at lunchtime to buy a sandwich and another drink. It is very easy to see how them not going in to work amounts to dire predictions for the future of the economy. The window cleaner was here yesterday, he reckons that he has lost half his customers because some people don't want him near their houses. I can't see what is wrong with him being up a ladder and outside, not much of a threat. Pubs don't want him, because they can't afford him, which is fair enough. A neighbour has been cutting back an overgrown hedge and throwing the bigger branches into our garden. The window cleaner asked me if he could pick some of the branches out for his log burner. 'Course you can.' Seemed to make his day.

***

There's this lady, a friend of ours, who comes one morning a week to help with the housework. She arrives before breakfast, when I am writing at the kitchen table. A good time for writing, early in the morning. Her first job is to make us both a cup of tea, it's my second of the day, she then sits down opposite me and lights a cigarette. I always put my pen down, take off my glasses, and ask her how things are going. 'Not good. I took the dogs out in the truck and the one won't get out; he's been there for two days. I can't get him out because he gets nasty.' I have never seen her dogs but know she has five: two German shepherds, two lurchers and a terrier. She takes them twice a day in her truck to some fields where she has permission to walk them. 'When I got back home the other day he wouldn't get out, even my son can't get him out.' 'Is he in there now?' 'Yes.' Later on I go to have a look. There's the biggest German Shepherd I have ever seen, stretched out on the back seat. He does not raise his head when I open the door. He just opens the eye that can see. He also opens his mouth so that I can see all his teeth and gives out this terrible growl. I shut the door. 'If you want to stay there, you stay just as long as you want.'

26 December 2020

The end of the year is as good a time as any to take stock. We know what stock we've got on the farm but we can only guess what wildlife is about. Top of my list are the hares. We have gone from having a lot to very few. The consensus of those of us about this farm is that in the spring we had four or five. The trouble with hares is that they are very difficult to count. You never know if you have seen the same hare twice or whether that is a different hare! Until they line up in an orderly fashion to do a roll call, I suspect that we are stuck with guessing. I remember that the first leverets we saw were a set of twins and whilst they were young we kept an eye on them. I also remember that I saw one of them being carried off by a red kite and because I never saw the other twin again, I assume it went the same way. It was fortunate that yesterday I bumped into the keeper who is a better wildlife counter than me. I've not seen him for a long time. He's only part time, his work situation has changed and he does his rounds at a different time of day to when I do mine. He tells me that he has seen a lot of hares in the woods. 'You had a nice lot here in the early autumn but the coursers have been twice and now there are very few.' Nature always astounds me with its ability to bounce back from adversity but I suspect we are back to single figures on hares. And they have the winter to get through first. If we have more than four or five, come the spring I shall be pleased, any less than that and we are going the wrong way.

But it gets worse. We have always had a flock of lapwings on this land, for twenty years probably, it has always been a small flock of between 12 and 18 birds. The irony is that for years we have put an area, six acres, into a lapwing-friendly mix of seeds that has included places for them to nest. I have been paid to do this, by the taxpayer. That taxpayer, be it British or European has paid. I have not seen a lapwing for 12 months!

I think red kites have seen them off. They eat their eggs and they eat their young and they just haven't bred. Thus they have probably died out. We used to see them wheeling above their chosen nesting ground, and on that ground there might be twenty red kites. Around the edges of that ground would be a similar number of buzzards and carrion crows; the red kites are the boss and the others are keeping a distance. You often see 'nature lovers' saying the widespread increases of red kites is a success story, and it is. But there has been a cost to that success, which is the decline of other species, and they rarely mention that.

***

Just when you think that things cannot get any worse, they usually do. We had a serious pre-Christmas crisis. The tree went up on the 2nd of December and then they couldn't find the lights! One of the downsides to living in a big old farmhouse, (apart from the cold), is that there is always room to dump stuff and so you never throw anything away. Our Christmas tree lights went in a black bin bag and joined lots of other black bin bags which lurk in passages, odd corners and attics. It took three days to find them. It's just as well because another day and Ann would have ordered new ones (her parents christened her without an 'E' on her name, in case she couldn't spell.) If you live in a house where space is at a premium, you are probably envious, but don't be. We have a bit of a clear-out every ten or fifteen years and we keep some of the stuff and it is still there when we have the next one, and we still haven't used it. There is a big old attic at the top of the house that I have not been in for twenty years. I think there is a troll living up there and we all know what happened to that Billy goat.

I used to say that I hated Christmas and a part of that was to be very grumpy in the run-up. I used to find that if you were really grumpy, you didn't get lots of hints as to what to buy people for presents, or even better, they didn't expect a present at all. Now I say that I really like it, which has thrown everyone. I have had two days staring at a naked tree, one without lights, and I've said that my Christmas is spoiled already, which has put everyone on the back foot. Much as they were when I was grumpy.

2 January 2021

People sometimes ask how many businesses rely on agriculture for their survival. The list is endless and I will not attempt it here. But if you should go to an agricultural show, those various businesses are all there on display. It is not just agriculture that this applies to. If a factory makes the headlines because it is closing with a big loss of jobs, they reckon there is just as big a loss of jobs elsewhere within the smaller firms that relied on that factory for work. What you do not see at an agricultural show is the evidence of all the people that are employed because of legislation. We are supposed to live in a paperless society but the paper that turns up on farms is endless and I am sure that more arrives than we had twenty years ago.

When a letter turns up at the farm, there is usually a cost to it. About ten years ago we agreed to take a course on the farm called a material handler proficiency course. It was designed so that we could drive our 4x4 loader more safely. It was mostly concerned with handling pallets but we usually use our machine to handle silage or muck, with a big shovel on the front.

We entered my son and the man who worked here at the time. We did not need to: they were both experienced operatives, but it was the responsible thing to do. Another farmer a few miles away also came to go through it. The course took five hours, three in the morning and two in the afternoon. The cost was £400 a person. So I had to pay £800 for our two places and it was £400 for the other farmer - goodness knows what it costs now. I remember thinking that the instructor had earned £1,200 for five hours work, I'm not saying it was all for him, it was for the organisation he worked for but that £800 was a lot of money then. I also remember that he saw me hanging about the yard and he said, 'Do you ever drive this?' I said yes, so he said 'I'll put you down for the course as well.'

He did not like it when I refused, he did not like it all. I asked our two participants what they had learnt and it didn't take them long to tell me! I did not notice any difference to how they drove after, either, but the important thing is that somewhere there are two pieces of paper that say that they passed. Where those pieces of paper are now, I have not got a clue. I spend most of my life looking for paper. If it's important I put it in a safe place, but where that safe place is, is anyone's guess.

***

Now we come to rats. Not an obvious link, but there you are. For reasons that are not clear to me there have been plenty of rats about this year. Not just on farms, in cities, everywhere. We have had trouble here. When we switched our central heating on in the autumn, it wouldn't work. We found that rats had chewed all the wiring on the boiler. The boiler is in a room that adjoins the house and a collie dog sleeps in there every night! There was a man here the other day, he calls here every month. We buy our dairy chemicals off him and he calls here for some money. Like most people who call here, he has become a friend.

Amongst all the things he sells, he also sells rat poison. I thought I would put some down. I thought that I would put some down so it would be waiting for the rats when they arrived. I suspect that rat poison is cheaper than having your central heating boiler rewired. He was telling me that he stocks some really effective rat poisons but he can't sell any of them to me because I haven't been on a rat poison course! I can buy rat poison from him but I can't buy the best.

Common sense tells me that if there are too many rats about, you need the very best poisons to control them. Cynicism tells me that there might be too many rats about because there is restricted access to the most efficient poisons!

I still think that there is nothing to beat some healthy, robust cats to control rats. If you want a cat to tackle a big rat, that cat needs to be fit and well, and keeping farm cats fit and well is not as easy as it sounds. You can rarely get within five yards of our farm cats, they are actually very wild, they just happen to live on our farm. My daughter had two young cats from the local cat rescue centre. Well, were they nasty! She does not ever remember stroking them. They used to put all that they killed on their doorstep every night. Rats and mice and birds but also stoats, weasels and squirrels. They called them the Kray twins.

My salesman friend is telling me about a farmer's son who paid to go on a rat poisoning course and therefore could access the best of poisons. He was so successful that he thought he would have a go at the moles. I should say at this point that if you get too much soil from moles hills in your silage, it can lead to listeria, which can kill your cattle. He tries to buy some stuff to put in the mole runs, but is told that he is only licenced for rats, mice and squirrels, if he wants to kill moles he has to pay to go on another course! Bureaucracy and red tape is alive and well in the countryside, along with the rats.

9 January 2021

My eldest granddaughter is in university. She has this boyfriend. He is a really nice lad but comes from a town that and has had no contact with farming. I can tell that farming intrigues him. It had never occurred to him that farmers worked such long hours and that it was the norm for farmers on livestock farms to work seven days a week. He is also much taken with our ability to laugh at adversity and to cope with what that life throws at us. Just lately he has taken to going to the gym regularly and because he had become so keen, he wanted to do some fitness training back at his student accommodation. They went one day to a sports shop and bought him a barbell so he could do some weightlifting at home. He buys this and says to my granddaughter, 'How are we going to get it home?' I was not there, obviously, but I bet she rolled her eyes, she is quite good at that. She picks up the barbell with one hand and carries it back the two miles to the university.

***

I have a good friend who is also a farmer. I call by to say hello about once a month. He has always got about five dogs about. My dog Gomer loves going there; when we turn down his lane Gomer is so delighted he can hardly contain his excitement. When we get there I have to let him out as soon as possible. They are all male dogs on that farm but they get on reasonably well. There is a little growling, much marking of territory, but once introductions are complete, they mix very well. My farmer friend has bought a new dog since we were last here. A breed called a Huntaway, they come from New Zealand or Australia, they are a big dog, brown and black, and are known for their barking when they work sheep or cattle. This particular dog is only yet half grown but he gives us a good demonstration of his ability to bark.

And so we talk about dogs. Have you noticed how dogs are such an important part of our lives? They are good companions and they create so much interest by just being there, with all their individual characteristics and their habits. I say how good natured his dogs all are. After all, this is their territory but Gomer is quite safe. It would be no surprise if they all ganged up on him. But they don't. He tells me that it wasn't always like this, that he once had a dog, a sheep dog, that was decidedly nasty. It used to bite someone, most days! If it could not find someone to bite on its own yard, it would travel further afield until it did. The trouble with this habit was that his nearest neighbour was also his landlord! This dog died when it was about three years old, it had a tumour. His landlord summed it up quite well. 'I'm very sorry that you have lost your dog but must admit that it's now much safer living around here.'

***

My next-door neighbour's partner is the best thing to arrive around here since I arrived myself. She makes me six dozen mince pies every Christmas. I don't think six dozen is enough since my grandsons have started eating them. She is very hard working. I went down there one morning and he was on the tractor, scraping the muck out, and she was on a squeegee, clearing the corners out by hand that he couldn't get to with the tractor. I always remember she said that she was living the dream. She usually does a lot of shoot lunches at this time of year, several a week. That had to stop because of covid restrictions but it has started again now. I was talking to her today and she told me that she often has to cater for a shoot party that includes vegetarians. She could not work out why a vegetarian would want to shoot pheasants. I cannot work it out either. Seems like some sort of contradiction there.

***

I know this is a delicate subject but being candid is important to me. It is to do with my dog Gomer. When he gets excited he always does a number two. I went to see a neighbour about a month ago and left him in my truck for an hour. I didn't let him out because these particular neighbours have a lot of dogs and they like to bite visitors. I feared for my own safety, let alone his. You are safe once you are sitting down at their kitchen table but there are usually two or three sheepdogs watching your every move, and you move your feet at your own peril. When I got back into the truck, Gomer had done a parcel on the back seat.

Next week I called to see another neighbour. They love dogs so I took him in. Sometime, when I was drinking coffee, he sneaked off and left his marker in their pantry. They were not a bit bothered.

We had two invitations out on Christmas day. In the morning we usually go for a drink at Jane's, (the florist friend) and in the early evening we go to my daughter's for our Christmas dinner. They have both found Gomer's 'little presents' in the past and this year they both said 'Don't bring that bloody dog with you!'

16 January 2021

It's a funny thing that around here no one takes any notice if you change your car but should you get a new working dog, everyone knows. In a way that puts life into a sort of perspective. It puts real value on a good dog. The world is full of good cars, but they are only cars. But a good working dog is hard to find and if you are lucky enough to find one they can give you untold pleasure.

I knew a neighbour had bought a new sheep dog that had cost a fair bit of money. He has a lot of sheep and a lot of dogs. I sometimes think that some farmers only keep sheep so that they can work sheep dogs. It's just like some farmers only farm so that they can drive a tractor. Anyway I ask this neighbour how his new dog is performing. I can tell straight away, by the look on his face, that he is disappointed. 'It's a Saturday sort of dog.' I've never heard this expression before so I ask him to explain. 'Well we don't do any big jobs with sheep on Saturdays and as he isn't very good and as we have plenty of time, we use him.'

Another neighbour said to me not long ago, 'You busy next Saturday, there's a dog I'd like to buy, I thought you could take me.' 'Where's the dog?' 'I can't remember, somewhere up north.' 'You will need to find out so we will know what time to start.' I think he asked me because around here I am considered quite widely travelled and I had a bigger, faster car than he did. I suspect that had something to with it. By the Friday morning I still hadn't heard where 'up north' we were bound, so I give him a ring. 'I can't remember but I'll phone now, I think it begins with H.' None the wiser I wait until he phones back, 'It's called Haw-wick'. I know where Hawick is: we used to play rugby up there on Fridays and then next day go on to watch Wales play Scotland in Edinburgh. 'We will need to start quite early, we have got to go up to Carlisle and then turn right.' As he has no idea where Carlisle is, this means nothing to him. It doesn't bother me how far it is, I like driving and I like a day out. My wife calls these trips a jolly, but that tends to underplay the seriousness of the occasion. When I turn up on his yard to collect him early on Saturday morning there are three other farmers there and they are also coming along for the ride and to oversee the buying of the dog.

I don't mind a bit and we enjoy the journey up the M6. We look at every field we pass and look at the livestock, which is what farmers do when they are travelling. Eventually we get to the farm. The man selling the dog is a shepherd on a big mixed farm.

We do not go to the dog for an hour because first of all he is interrogated by the other farmers. 'How big is this farm, how many cattle are there and how many sheep?' Each answer prompts another question and so it goes on. Finally we get to the dog. The dog is demonstrated but it's not much of a demonstration. There is a big flock of ewes folded on some roots and they can run back onto a grass field. The dog moves them back and fore ok, but as they are used to doing that every day, it isn't a real test. And so we finally get to it. 'How much did you want for him?' 'I told you on the phone.' They both seem reluctant to make a start. Eventually the shepherd says '£2,000' There is much shuffling about from the audience and looks are exchanged. 'I'll give you £700.' I give an inward groan, I have been on the wrong end of my friend's long range negotiations before and know full well how long they can take. We could be here for ages. Perhaps we will need bed and breakfast!

After about half an hour they agree on £770. This is a surprise to me and it could have been done quicker if they had just talked properly to each other in the first place.

The light is fading when we start for home but the traffic is light, the car is going well and you can do a long way on a motorway in a couple of hours. It isn't quite so interesting as the journey up, because it's now dark but by the time the passengers have discussed the dog, the shepherd and where he lives we have covered many a mile. Then about fifty miles from home we see a pub's lights up ahead and someone in the back says the fateful words, 'I think it's about time we tried one.' That dog was never much good, in fact £70 would have been plenty for him. That was probably why the shepherd came down on his price so quickly. Still it was a day out, even if it was a long one. Good working dogs are hard to find. One of the troubles is, folk rarely sell one.

23 January 2021

I know a man who is widely known as being a very good and safe shot with his rifle he has. He gets a call to go to deal with a fox that is creating a problem on an isolated farm. The problem is, the fox has moved into their garden shed. It comes out at night, it goes scavenging around the farm buildings, and now they do not have as many farm cats as they used to have. Then it turns over their wheely bins. It spends what is left of the night on their lawn, chewing their children's plastic toys to the point of destruction. The children, for their part, are afraid to play in the garden because they know the fox is in the shed.

The man takes his rifle to the farm and in due course goes out into the garden. The fox hears him about and comes out of the shed to see what is going on. The fox sits down, much as a dog would do, and shows no fear. The rifle is used, the fox is examined and found to be in excellent condition. This was,

without doubt, a fox that had been caught in a city and dumped
in the countryside: where else would it learn to be so tame? There
is a lot of anti fox hunt stuff in the media at present. I have never
been fox hunting but I've seen too much to have much sympathy
with foxes. I have been on the wrong end of fox activity too often.
To most livestock farmers, they are just another pest. It seems
that people who live in towns feel the same way.

***

It has not been a good time to run a rugby club. Especially not
if your main source of income is usually the bar. Drinking with
a substantial meal does not really do it for rugby clubs like ours.
Traditionally it has been almost the other way around: a plate of
chips and substantial drinking! A man I know, who is known to
like his drink, was here the other day so I asked him how he was
managing under this meal-only regime. He said that he had been
in a pub the day before and had had plenty to drink, (and believe
me, when he says plenty, he means plenty) but he had taken 4½
hours to eat a pizza! The rugby club has bought a marquee. The
idea is that is you have more room, you can put more tables in
and thus more people and when things eventually get going, sell
more drink.

***

I am a bit of an expert on marquees. The club was given a big
one years ago and I took charge of it. It was a two poler. This was
at a time before marquees went portable frame, and the wealth
of a farmer was judged by how many poles there were in the
marquee at his daughter's wedding. 'Boy, he must be worth a bit,
there were four poles in the tent at his daughter's wedding.' My
daughter had her reception in a marquee on our lawn. Barclays
bank paid for that but they didn't know, nor did they find out!
The first time we put the club tent up was for my son's wedding.
He had his reception here as well. We badly underestimated just

how big the tent was. Our main lawn used to be a tennis court, so we thought it was plenty big enough but the corners of the tent had to be lashed to branches of trees. I will always remember that we had a local live band in the evening. We also had a turkey stag called Boris at that time and he joined the band on stage and danced along as they played.

***

Our main use for the rugby club marquee was for our annual dinners. We soon found out that it was big enough if we put it up with just one pole and the two ends. There was room to sit 120-130 people and plenty of room for the bar and caterers.

I remember that I once hired it out to a friend who was having a pedigree cattle sale. We had to put it up in a paddock next to his yard. During the evening when we put it up, someone left a trial of footprints of the brown stuff that comes out of cows all across what was the inside of the ceiling canvas. Those footprints remained there to be seen for just as long as we had that tent. I used to look at them at formal dinners when we all had our suits on and above us on the ceiling were cow muck footprints. But there was also a fondness there as well. There has always been a place for a farmer with dirty boots at our rugby club.

We hired the rugby club marquee out to a farmer friend of mine in Craven Arms who was selling his dairy herd. We put the marquee up in his orchard and on the day I went to the auction he held in it, along with my son and a good friend. The sale went well and after the sale there was a bit of a party.

When we decided it was prudent to go we decided we shouldn't drive so we phoned home for my daughter to come and fetch us. After she had been there an hour we had to phone my wife to fetch the four of us home!

30 January 2021

I have not mentioned TB for a long time but it is no wonder it gets farmers so wound up. Here is where we are. We sent off two old cows in September, one of these was deemed as warranting further investigation and some of her tissue was sent off to a laboratory. We were 'closed down', which means we can't sell any calves, which is fair enough. Shortly after that we had our whole herd routine test. At that test they found three of what they call 'inconclusives', which means that they didn't pass the test, but neither did they fail it. These three were tested again after sixty days and then they passed. We've still not heard how the first cow got on at the laboratory. That's four months that we have not been able to sell calves. More importantly we don't know if we have TB or not. We are short of room, short of fodder, short of the money that would bring in. But there is no rush, apparently.

**

The countryside intrigues me, you have probably worked that out by now, but what is happening now and what will happen soon is new to all of us. The most numerous birds around here in the late summer and autumn are the pheasants. They are released in their thousands by shoots, and eventually they are shot in their thousands as well. But, like a lot of things, the shooting comes to an end, and many of the pheasants are still there. What will happen to them? Normally the pheasants that are left are fed wheat in the hard months of February and March. There is little else for them to eat. This is a good thing. If there is a hard snow and you go into a wood, you will find lots of small birds there as well. They will be close to a pheasant feeder and the wheat that is meant for pheasant keeps them alive as well.

But like lots of things, shoots now have their financial problems. Wheat is very expensive so there is a dilemma: do we feed all these pheasants? If we don't, they will die. I have heard the suggestion that the shooting season will be extended into February but I can't see that happening. Nature follows the seasons and all birds will be making arrangements to breed. Pheasants that have been reared are notoriously bad breeders. They lay eggs ok but it is very rare to see a hen pheasant rear her young. Winged predators are the main threat. It is only my conjecture but I think that most of these pheasants will be caught up and their final destination will be a plate, which is where they were headed anyway.

***

My next door neighbour's partner made me eight dozen mince pies for Christmas. It takes some serious eating to get through eight dozen. I don't usually eat anything at midday but my wife is home more now and we are in lockdown and she brings me a cup of tea whilst I watch the 1 o'clock news. Just lately she has brought me a mince pie as well, then she started to bring me two. Her argument was that there were mince pies everywhere and that I had got to eat them. Yesterday I was eating the first one and contemplating eating the second, I don't need two mince pies but I also like a quiet life and you have to balance it all up. The second mince pie is on a plate and the plate is on a stool next to my arm chair. Then I hear a faint noise and look down in time to see my dog Gomer, who is on his hind legs, take the second mince pie and carry it off. I get crumbs everywhere eating mine but he eats his on the carpet and there's not a crumb to be seen. Now, when he gives me one of his sad looks, a look that says, 'Let's go for a ride in the truck,' I tell him that I don't want a thief in my truck.

***

There is a piece in our daily paper about the authenticity of one of the Victoria Crosses awarded at Rourke's Drift. Most of us know that story well because we have watched the film *Zulu*. When the film came out it was quite scary, with all those Zulus coming over the hills. I introduced my two eldest grandsons to it when they were little boys and they watched it from behind the settee. It also provided one of my favourite funny stories. When the film first came out, we went with some friends to see it at a cinema. We have not been to the cinema very often in our married life. Anyway, we're at the height of the battle and you can't see how the soldiers can possibly hold out any longer as wave after wave of Zulu's hurl themselves at the makeshift barricades. It's nail-biting stuff and my friends wife leans across to me and says very seriously, 'The bugler doesn't get killed because he lives next door to my Granny in Brecon.'

6 February 2021

Now that I can't go to the pub on Saturdays, I spend the evening reading but the television is always on as well. At some time during the evening they give out the winning numbers of the National Lottery. It is something I had forgotten about. There is a sort of competition in the pub to do with the bonus ball. I pulled out of that about three years ago, you had the same number every week and you paid a £1 a week, I had not won for two years so I came out. But it is years ago now since the real lottery started and I remember being quite enthusiastic about that. All our cows have numbers so I said that my lottery numbers would be chosen by the first cows in the parlour. That's how I chose my numbers but I can report that my cows were no good at choosing lottery numbers!

But there is a story there as well. I went to the Royal Welsh Show and at shows the best hospitality is usually found at the stands that sell semen to be used in artificial insemination on dairy cows. I must have availed myself too much of the hospitality on offer because I ordered 12 doses of a breed I had never used before, Brown Swiss.

Normally if you have 12 doses of semen you can expect about six pregnancies and thus three heifer calves (on the basis that you will get a 50/50 split on sexes born). I got 12 pregnancies and nine heifer calves!

I remember the first one born particularly, she grew into a big black cow and she was the boss cow by some distance. She was always first in the parlour, the other cows would not go off to graze unless she went first, neither would they come home to be milked unless she led the way. We knew her as No14 and she was first on my lottery numbers. I only tell you this because if you do numbers you might want to think again. Most people, when they think of the lottery, think of winning large amounts of life changing money but when I hear mention of the word lottery, I think of a big black cow.

***

I know it is not a laughing matter but if I had £1 for every time I have seen on TV someone getting a vaccine in their arm, I could go to the pub more often. If it were open. And if I had another £1 for every time I have seen an expert on the pandemic who was also a professor, I could start drinking in the lounge bars. I had never realised that there were so many professors about! Is there a collective noun for a lot of professors? They don't seem to have any good news, so it could be a gloom of professors. Not that I want to go into lounge bars anyway. Real people are mostly found in the public bar.

Years ago I had a friend who made a lot of hay in those conventional bales. This meant that there was a lot of hard work involved in getting them safely into the barns. He was very good at getting help at weekends to shift all these bales. He used to say 'you'll never find someone to help you shift bales in a lounge bar'. This saying of his was more eloquent than it first appears. It is a profound comment on life itself. Think about it.

As I write, there is a huge rush to get everyone vaccinated. That way, we are told, lies the only way out of the present mess. And so there is a big rush on, there is a rush to get stocks of vaccine in the right place and there is a rush to get lots of people in place to inject the actual vaccine. Retired nurses and doctors are wanted and they are even training staff at your local pharmacy. But I cannot help but think that the government are missing a trick here. Farmers are well used to administering injections, so why not use them? It is true there would have to be a few changes made. Farmers use the same syringe time and time again. And those NHS needles would need upgrading to something thicker and more robust for farmers.

The more you think about it, the better it is. If you are vaccinating sheep, for example, you can buy vaccine in a sort of satchel that you put on your back. There is a long tube that takes the vaccine in a sort of gun that is used to do the actual vaccination, and the gun is replenished after each injection. Just imagine: you could get say two hundred people in a line with their sleeves rolled up and go down that line and vaccinate them in no time at all. It wouldn't suit the faint-hearted; you would need to be quite brave to get into that line in the first place. For some people there would be no more a chilling sight than a farmer approaching them, probably in dirty overalls, brandishing a syringe. Using a sheep vaccination kit I could probably do one thousand a day and I am available. To get the best results a new sheep handling set up would be handy, I could put humans through there.

13 February 2021

I recently stood in the village as the funeral car came by for a good friend who lived locally and was an agricultural engineer. That is just about as close as you can get to attending a funeral these pandemic days, if you are not family. He had done really well in life, I can remember him starting out on his own. His workshop was his garage in his garden. Now he has purpose-built premises on an industrial estate and employs several people and is a main dealer for tractors and machinery. He had done well because he was always straight and always in a good humour and I used to think that his success was built on the respect people had for him. He always used to call me 'Rogery lad' which I used to like and I shall miss.

But I'm not about to write an eulogy, I'm about to write about bales. You will see lot of bales on your travels, and they will have two things in common: they are quite big and they are moved by the hydraulic power of tractors and loaders. When big bales came on the scene it was a major thing in farming.

Previously all that hay and straw was put into small bales and moved by hand. It was a lot of work, I know because I did a lot of it. The irony was that if it was a bad year weather-wise, the bales would be heavier and every time you lifted one you would know, by the weight if it, that it was of indifferent quality.

But the balers that made those small conventional bales didn't all get scrapped when they became obsolete. There are many of them tucked away in the corner of a shed. Their owners still like to get them out if there is a prolonged spell of dry weather, it's a sort of comfort thing. I like having a few small bales about – they are handy if you out a cow in a box to calve on Sunday afternoons or to sell a few to that girl down the village for her pony. So they get these old balers out, dust them off and grease them, and pray that the knotters still work.

I did a lot of conventional baling but the worst thing that could go wrong was the knotters. If only one of the two worked, the bales would bend until they broke up, and you would have to carry all this loose hay back around and put it through the baler again. I wasn't any good at faulty knotters, there was a snap to them that spelt lost fingers but this friend of mine was an expert, Farmers used to say that if you got your small baler out and the knotters were playing up, he was the man. He often used to invite me to call in for a chat and I had every intention to do just that, but I have left it too late. Just as I left it too late to call for a chat with the man who told me he had been to a hiring fair as a youth; and the man who had worked with horses on farms all his working life. Have I learnt how precious memories are? Apparently not. I'm sure that there are books somewhere that would do the same job but there can be no substitute for learning about this living history face to face and first-hand from people you know. My memory is of riding on a baler, watching those knotters. No safe seat, lots of dust, all that machinery going around. Not a high vis jacket in sight, no health and safety. I tend to be very cautious about safety on the farm now, possibly because I can remember all the risks we used to take.

***

On our yard we have this shed where we calve our cows. It is our biggest shed and it's very central to what we do on a daily basis. There is human activity about there all day long. My two eldest grandsons live about twenty yards away. They live in what they call a mobile home but I call it a love nest. We have two farm dogs and they are about there all day as well.

Calving sheds are very attractive to dogs. There is the detritus from the actual calvings, placenta and the like, and calves that are only having milk off their dams have bright yellow faeces that is much sought after and eaten by dogs. That is a good reason why you should never let a farm dog lick your face. There is a fox lives in this shed as well, at least at night he lives there. Every morning he is to be seen leaving the shed leisurely as the day's activity increases. He makes his way, without any hurry, to a hedge about fifty yards away where he has a nice cosy place to sleep. No one sees him come back but he is always there again next morning. He is without doubt another town fox that has been dropped off, why else would he be so tame? There have been rumours here for some time that a number of town foxes have been dropped off in the area, and it looks as if we have one. At the moment he's not doing any harm so we live and let live.

20 February 2021

I know we shouldn't wish our lives away but I am not sorry to see the end of January. January, as a month, has very little to commend it, but January under lockdown is best forgotten. I used to like going to the pub on Sunday nights in January, there only used to be five or six of us there and as we had all been there on Saturday night as well, there was rarely anything new for anyone to say. We used to say that a lot of people couldn't go to the pub on Sunday nights in January because they couldn't afford it, they were still paying for Christmas. I couldn't really afford it but there is only you and me know that. When I look back, the only thing to commend the pub in January is that it is warmer than our house.

February, on the other hand, is different, there are signs of spring to be seen. There are signs in January but they are often misleading. The first flower of the year arrives, the snowdrop. They arrive anyway, whatever the weather and however dark the day. They usually get covered with snow and frost. If they are a sign heralding a new start, it is best disregarded. I have always thought the snowdrops were stupid plants anyway. My neighbour has had lambs in his fields since Christmas. Surely that is a sign of spring. But these lambs have been wandering about in snow, just lately. They look as if they wish they were still inside their mothers and who can blame them? Over their heads fly buzzards and red kites, you can almost see them licking their lips (or beaks).

They circle like vultures in a cowboy Western when someone has left a dead horse somewhere.

***

When I kept sheep I used to lamb them in March but there was one exception. I remember one Christmas day, I had finished all my jobs in good time. I remember the milk tanker had come an hour early, so I thought I would walk down and see the sheep. This was all part of my impression of having to work all day which in turn was part of my impression of being in a bad mood. I used to have a bad habit that when I went to market in the spring, I would walk amongst the selling ewes and lambs, just to see if there was anything a bit different for sale. One year I bought an unusual ewe and lamb. She was a Manx Loaghtan, at least I think she was, she looked more like a goat. She was here for a number of years and when I shore her she had a nice brown wool underneath.

But I also bought one of my favourites, one year. I bought a Dorset Horn ewe and two lambs. And when I am strolling amongst my sheep on this Christmas morning, I come across the Dorset ewe and she has hooked one of her horns in the fence and can't get free. She was hooked herself quite high up on the wire netting and cannot even lie down. This is a surprise as she was ok when I went around the sheep the day before, but it is quite muddy where she, is so I suspect she has been there all night. But there is an even bigger surprise: at her feet are two lambs. They are warm, they have full bellies and are fine. I get the ewe free and she makes a fuss of her lambs – until now she couldn't get her head low enough to lick them.

That is my only experience of early lambing. People will tell you that Dorset ewes will lamb twice a year but, in my experience (and I should know because if you have one, that's experience), they usually lamb three times in two years. I always had a soft spot for Dorsets; they were easy to manage, they were milky and good mothers. Perhaps if I ever bought some more it would be better to buy some without horns. That is unlikely to happen. My son doesn't like sheep, if I bought some he would be gone next day.

***

I know a man who used to manufacture luxury motor boats. He used to sell them all over the world and he had sales representation at marinas on the Mediterranean and in Florida. He sold a boat to a lady in Florida. Just to put some perspective on this, it was about twenty years ago, the boat was half a million pounds and she ordered about £150,000 of extras on top of that. Goodness knows what that would cost today! Anyway, whilst the boat was being built they asked her if she wanted Volvo or Cumming engines. She replied that she wanted neither, she had no intention of ever taking the boat to sea. She had bought it so that she could have drinks parties on the marina!

27 February 2021

Most people could do without a lockdown. I could do without it but we all have to make the best of it. I have superb views to look at and I never tire of them. I have not been in a shop or a pub for weeks now, but neither have I been in my wallet! I put some cash in there before Christmas and as far as I know it is still there. There is nowhere to go and very little to do but I have a saying, 'Everything in life is relative.' There was a lady on a news programme I watched the other night. She lived on the fifteenth floor of a tower block with three children of primary school age. She was cheerful, as were her children. The children were polite and well behaved. She said she was one of the lucky ones because her flat had a balcony so had access to fresh air, whereas a lot of her neighbours didn't have a balcony. The balcony was not as big as our kitchen table. Some of us are luckier than others. Sometimes there is little we can do about it, but we should acknowledge our luck.

***

Pheasants are released around here in large numbers in late summer and early autumn for shooting. They are a commonplace sight but their behaviour when shooting finishes always intrigues me. They always seem to know within a couple of days, when the season is finished and they are safe. And their behaviour becomes bolder as a consequence. It is all more interesting this year because shooting finished early, because of lockdown, and there are more pheasants about now, at this time of year, than there have ever been. There's a group of over twenty that visit our garden every day, I don't know where they come from or where they roost. A group of pheasants can travel a long way on their daily adventures.

***

We still have cattle outside. We grow about six patches of cover crops for the shoot; kale and the like. We usually graze them off in March when the heifers go out but these crops are well past their best by then. As they are not now wanted by the shoot, we are grazing them now. A month ago my son was moving some heifers from one patch to another. He parks his truck by the buildings and sets off on foot to get the heifers. A cock pheasant tucks in behind him. You often get cock pheasants walking with you later on, in spring. They have usually taken exception to you striding into what they consider their breeding territory. They will accompany you aggressively, often pecking at your heels, until they no longer consider you a threat and then they will hot foot it back to their 'spot', where they have hens secreted in the hedgerows.

This particular cock pheasant did none of that. He accompanied my son on his fairly long walk, very much as your dog would walk with you. He watched him move the cattle. My son has a great gift for moving cattle on his own. He never takes the dog, except to fetch the cows for milking, and he declines all offers for help with dry cows and heifers – no dog, no stick and no swearing. The family think he is some sort of cow whisperer but we have never told him.

The cock pheasant is an interested spectator to all this and when they have moved the cattle, he accompanies my son back to his truck. Altogether the moving of the cattle has taken possibly an hour and a half and covered about three miles. My son gets into his truck and returns home and the cock pheasant goes back to whatever cock pheasants do when there is no shooting and it is too early to mate.

My son goes to see the same cattle every day at about the same time but he never sees the cock pheasant again, at any rate, not as a walking companion. I suspect that the pheasant thought he was the keeper and was about to dispense feed. When he didn't, I suspect the pheasant thought his long walk was a complete waste of time and now spends his time in the woods next to a wheat feeder. Why some people will pay money to shoot such tame birds remains a mystery to me.

***

There is a lady, a friend of ours, who comes one morning a week to help with the housework. She always comes early and her first job is to make me a cup of tea and to sit down and we have a gossip. She is quick of temper and she has very little patience, but it is best not to remind her of this. She says that she was a naughty girl the day before. She has a horse and she had to put the horse box onto her truck to fetch a big round bale of hay. She has a four-wheel trailer and one axle was frozen. She decides that if she drives off it will free itself. But it doesn't, so she drives faster. In the end she drives so fast that all she can see in the mirror is blue smoke. Eventually she hears the tyres burst. Two new tyres cost her £100. I don't know how much that bale of hay cost her. Best not to ask.

6 March 2021

These last years I have taken an interest in politics and I always read the letter if Ian Liddell-Grainger is in Saturday's *Western Daily Press*. I think it is important to hear what MPs in rural constituencies are thinking. I don't know much about Mr Liddell-Grainger but I saw him ask a question on Prime Minister's question time last week and if I couldn't contrive a better question than that, I wouldn't bother the Prime Minister with it. I am always intrigued by the fact that his letter is to DEFRA boss George Eustace. They are of the same party, don't they ever speak? I have got mixed feelings about Mr Eustace, he looks too pleased with himself for my liking, probably because he has been promoted beyond his wildest dreams. I wonder if he has come to terms with the fact that the Prime Minister's fiancé has more influence over rural affairs than he has. To be fair to him, he was at least elected. Mr Liddell-Grainger was advocating the use of electric collars on dogs as means to stop livestock worrying. I differ with his opinion. Does he think that people who let their dogs off the lead when there are livestock about or who let their dogs stray, are going to buy an E-collar?

I was once invited for a day out on quite a posh shoot. I only knew the host, I didn't know any of the other guns. One of those guns had a young dog to which he had fitted an electric collar. The dog was quite headstrong and every time it did something wrong, which was quite often, it received an electric shock. I found its yelps of pain quite upsetting. I always think that a badly behaved dog reflects more on the owner than it does on the dog. At the end of the first drive I told my host I was going home. 'Going home' has a particular resonance on a shoot. There are very strict protocols to observe on a shoot and if the host asks a guest to go home, it is the ultimate indignity. It is very unusual for a guest, as I was doing, to dismiss himself.

Obviously I was asked why, and I said that I wasn't going to spend the rest of the day watching that poor dog being ill-treated. Others of the guns heard this exchange and agreed with me so it wasn't me that went home, it was the man with the dog with the E-collar. No, Mr Liddell-Grainger, I do not agree with you, I think these collars are cruel, I don't think they will do what you think, and I think they should be banned. That's not to say that livestock worrying is not a serious issue. I think it will get worse, simply because there are more dogs about and people can't accept the fact that their pet, who is one of the family, can be so vicious.

***

I once bought a yellow lab pup, we called him Laddie. He had two faults. If you let him in to watch TV he would shed hairs on the carpet; and he would chase sheep. He didn't bite the sheep, he just chased them until one of them flopped down exhausted and he would lie on it and lick it's face. We thought so much of him in all other respects that I sent him away to a dog trainer. When he came back he was still chasing sheep. There are lots of sheep around here and I had to have him put down. Dogs that chase sheep but don't actually bite them can cause the greatest loses. They can chase sheep into corners and they get on top of each other and suffocate. The worst case I know personally was where there was a field that was accessed by a track that was about 12 feet lower, there was a sort of cutting in the corner that led down to the gate. Dogs chased the sheep into this corner and they piled on top of each other. When they removed the dead sheep they were ten deep in some places and 86 were dead. Not one sheep had a bite on it.

***

I've got a better idea, why don't we fit these collars to MPs? If they were on TV and we thought that they were not answering a question, or just waffling or even lying, we could press a button on our remote and give them an electric shock. A zap around the neck would soon bring them to heel. The only downside I can think of is that your remote would need a new battery every day.

***

I have been for my jab. Lots of people say, 'How did you get on?' I always say that the doctor said it was the nicest arm she had ever seen. It really annoys people, especially my family. I used to go to the doctors with an injury and the family would say, 'How did you get on with your knee.' And I would say that the doctor said it was the nicest knee he had ever seen and that he had called all the people from the waiting room to have a look as well. I get some perverse pleasure from winding people up, but only on issues that really don't matter.

13 March 2021

When the children were young and we took them on holiday by the sea, I would always go for a walk after tea, to look at the boats. Sea fishing is so fascinating, you don't know what is going to come up next in a pot or net. It might seem a bit of a stretch but I have always thought that sea fishing and farming had a lot in common. We both have the same sort of social issues. People buying our local houses as second homes or to retire to. Both farmers and fishermen can have good years or bad years, according to the weather. Fishing would appear to be more dangerous but statistics of accidents in farming, particularly handling livestock, are bad. You have to invest large sums in both; the cost of some of the boats seems astronomical. Europe brought us both quotas. Now we are both expected to operate sustainably by a population that knows very little about how things 'work'. I recently saw one of those UK travel programmes where the celebrity presenter visited a large estate that was being let go to run wild. 'This is the future,' she said breathlessly. Never mind that the large estate had been in the same family for generations and therefore had no rent to pay and no bank manager to satisfy. Never mind that there are now about 60 million people in this country and if all the land were let go like that, it would feed about 10-20 million. How would you feed the rest – import it?

However, I digress, climbing off one of my hobby horses I return to fishing. Farming and fishing are both political footballs, and the future of both depends on politicians, which is a bit of a worry.

***

I remember once we were on holiday and we were mackerel fishing. It was only a small boat and our family filled it. After I had got them all fishing I sat myself down by the skipper, who was steering at the rear with a tiller. At first, conversation was hard work; he was polite enough but he didn't contribute much to the conversation. Then I told him that I was a farmer and he changed completely, he asked me about my life and I asked him about his. One of the questions I asked him was what he did in the winter. 'Shoot seagulls,' he replied, without hesitation. Of course I wanted to know how he did that. He told me that there was a landfill refuse site close by and he and two friends were employed by the council to shoot seagulls. (The more discerning of you will have noted that I haven't told you where we are). What they used to do was drive a very old refuse lorry into the site, the seagulls would flock around, and two of them, in the back of the lorry would shoot some. I've always said that if a species becomes too numerous it needs some human control to bring the numbers back into balance. Most people think there are too many seagulls about. There are seagulls around here that have never been to the seaside and are therefore not to be trusted.

***

Not a big fan of seagulls, me. I was attacked by one once in Cardiff on my way to a rugby match. I was crossing a road and didn't see it coming. It hit me in the face and I nearly went down. My companions caught me and prevented that. They are used to catching me when I stumble at 11 o'clock at night but not at 11am in the morning! The seagull had a rest on a ledge above a shop window.

To complete the fishing theme, here's a story of my own. We were once on holiday on an island off the west coast of Scotland. Everyone had gone shopping but I went for a mooch around the quay. I saw a fishing boat come in so I went to have a look. They were sorting their catch so I sat down on some boxes to watch. They had been after langoustines and were sorting them into trays. Two men got out of a nearby car and boarded the boat. I can't remember if they wore uniforms but I took them to be some sort of fishery officers. They checked the count, checked some for size and then went on their way.

Now here's the strange thing. At no time did anyone speak. There were no hellos, no goodbyes. The air was full of the smell of the sea, and resentment. I found it all very strange; after all these men probably met most days. We get officials on farms. On this farm we try to jolly them along and get a good relationship. The rest of the family think that this is best achieved by keeping me out of sight. We, as farmers, get grants for all sorts of things, like helping wildlife for example. If they so wanted, these officials could fine you. You would not have to pay the fine, they would just deduct it from what they owed you. Good job we don't sell langoustines.

20 March 2021

On Saturday I'm looking at the view from our farmhouse window. It's the same view, it only varies with the seasons, but it's a lovely view and I never tire of it. About fifty to one hundred yards away is our pond and beyond that is a line of trees that I planted on some boggy ground. I can only see about thirty yards of the trees but today they are of interest. There are six or seven red kites in the trees, they are there all day, and they are busy. They are continuously flying in and out but I can't see what they are doing. Something has attracted them but I can't see what.

There is a pair of Canada geese nesting on the island in the pond but the kites usually clear their offspring out when they are a week old. What do you think they were up to? People who think they know best tell us that kites are scavengers and only eat carrion, but their population has gone way beyond what dead animals will support.

The birds and mammals that suffer their predations are numerous, for example, I haven't seen a lapwing for eighteen months now. I grow six acres of lapwing cover every year, the taxpayer pays for it, but it's my choice. What a waste of money. The kite is a beautiful bird but boy they do some damage. The only way we could satisfy the present population of kites is if we left dead farm animals about the fields for them to eat. But we are not allowed to do that.

The demise of the high street and its shops is well chronicled. It reminded me of when I once did some shopping. We were in a department store in Torquay. My wife had a serious shopping demeanour about her, I knew she would be some time, so I found a chair, plonked myself down, and proceeded to watch the world go by. My attention was drawn to a nearby rack which was full of coloured blazers. These blazers, or so a notice told us, were seriously reduced in price. I remember thinking they were a bargain but I didn't need a blazer. Then I saw a notice at the cash desk that said that anyone taking out a store loyalty card would get 50% discount on their first purchase.

Then I thought that if I took out a loyalty card and used it to get one of those blazers, it would be really cheap and that's what I did. I nearly changed my mind, filling the forms out took longer than it does to buy a tractor on the HP and the detail they wanted was a bit intrusive, but I didn't have anything else to do. Eventually I got my card and bought a dark green blazer. It cost me £10 but I only wore it once. I wore it was at a 'do' at the rugby club. In the car park someone said that a) they didn't know I played golf and b) they didn't know that I played it so well that I had obviously just won the US Masters. I had similar comments all evening.

The blazer spent the next ten years in my wardrobe and then I had a bit of a clear out and gave it to a man who was working for us. He thought it was really cool. I thought that I was quite clever to buy a new blazer for £10 but I wasn't as clever as I thought, we rarely are. I paid £10 just to wear it once. And I never used the store card again.

***

I've just had a birthday. My eldest granddaughter asks if I would like her to take me out for lunch. I said yes immediately, I didn't give it any thought. If she told me to jump off a cliff I would consider it. When I get into her car it's full of balloons, hadn't expected that. Then I have to put on what she calls 'party' sunglasses, which are in the form of two big daisies. Just hope we don't see anyone I know. She switched her phone on. It's playing a song that is a favourite in our family, 'Alice's Restaurant'. I hadn't given any thought to where we would go, not with everything shut. Going to a McDonalds drive thru was not on my wish list but that's where we went and I'll tick it off now that I've been to one. It was very busy, everyone seemed to know what to do and where to go. Not sure I could negotiate it on my own. 'You can get everything you want at Alice's Restaurant,' the song went. Bit like McDonalds.

27 March 2021

I just love trees. In all my years as a farmer I have only cut down one live tree. I'm quite proud of that. Contrary to popular belief about farmers, I've never removed a hedge either. I cut down the one live tree the year we moved in here. There was a sycamore growing close to the kitchen window and if it had fallen down it would have brought most of the house down with it. The insurers made me fell it. If the same situation arose today, drastic tree surgery would have done the job.

***

We have a five-acre field in front of our house, like a bit of park land. It used to be full of trees. Seventeen trees died in the drought of 1976. I planted seventeen trees to replace them. Planting trees is the easy bit, but then you have to protect them. You put those plastic thingys around them to keep the rabbits from barking them. Then a much bigger job, and more expensive, is to protect them from sheep and cattle. We made a tidy job of this, or so we thought, but unfortunately we had a Limousin bull at the time who thought it was his mission in life to destroy these tree guards. It takes a particularly robust tree guard to resist the aggressive attentions of over a ton of bull. After the bull had done his worst, the cows would go in and browse the young tree until there was only a bit of stem left. And it would die.

We did our best to repair the guards but the trouble with farming is that you sometimes can't leave what you are doing. For example, you can't stop harvesting to mend a tree guard. I was very glad when that particular bull went and the problem went with him. Out of the seventeen trees we planted, I think that there are now 12 trees left that are big enough to look after themselves.

And all is not lost. Centrepiece of this field is our pond. I suspect it started life as a small quarry and the spoil was put around it to catch the water that seeped out of the rock. Below the pond is a boggy area. When the cows went into it they used to go up to their hocks in the mud and get their udders dirty and I would have to wash them clean at milking time. I fenced the boggy area off and planted 25 trees. Whilst I was at it, I identified three or four more places around the farm where there were odd corners where I could put short fences in and plant trees. If I did it all now I would get a grant towards doing it, so I was ahead of my time! The trees below the pond are getting so big I have booked a tree surgeon to take them down a bit. They are taking my view when I sit in my armchair. It's not that I am nosy. (I am very nosy).

Our next big tree planting exercise came when we went into chickens. It was part of planning permission that we had to plant trees around the perimeter. We planted 2,000 and they have been there about twenty years now. They are now so big that from about 400 yards away it look like a two-acre wood. Those that know the chicken sheds are there can't see them and have forgotten they are there and those that don't know, well, they just don't know.

My favourite trees are the weeping willow and the cedar. I've had two or three goes at growing weeping willows. They are still there but they have never come to much. They start to look promising and then their leaves seem to be affected by a sort of blight and die off, and that is the end of that for another year. I've been told that I should spray them but there is always something more urgent to do on a farm. My daughter has a superb weeping willow at her farm. It grows so well it tries to block the entrance to her house. Every four years or so, my son-in-law takes his chain saw to it and cuts every branch off. All that is left is the trunk but next year back it comes again to start another cycle.

We have a cedar tree in our garden. Some years ago a storm split it and took two thirds of it so what is left is not a thing of beauty. We've just put an owl nesting box in it. I know that we should have put the box in a barn but I can see the entrance to the box from the kitchen table. I don't know yet if it's worked but I have heard more owl activity out there this winter. I haven't gone to shine torches at it in case there are birds there and I scare them off. I can wait until the nights get lighter. If there are owls there, we will see them then and I do think there are tawny owls in there. I was hoping for barn owls. Is there a bird anywhere in this country with more beautiful plumage? Still, tawny owls are a start.

3 April 2021

I know that I use it myself occasionally, about once every two months, and I know that people have to use it with all those shops shut and expect it will become a norm in our lives. I refer to the modern phenomenon of parcels being delivered by white vans. There were three here yesterday. There is one here most days because my two eldest grandsons do all their shopping online and buy bits and pieces most days. The parcels get delivered to our house and ends up on our kitchen table. I ask my wife what's in each package. 'They are not for you.' Is there anyone anywhere who is not curious if there is a parcel about? My eldest grandson opens the largest parcel that came yesterday, it was about the size of an A4 sheet on the top and about six inches deep. 'What was in there?' She says, 'Mind your own business.' He says 'a birthday card.' It wasn't a big birthday card, it was just the normal size. Why did it need such a big box and so much packaging? The advent of the white van and all that packaging is hardly a green answer to anything! How times have changed. When we first came here, our postman came on a bike. We were putting out first milking parlour in then and all the electric motors and the heavy bits and pieces came in the post. He was a bit grumpy about it and blamed me personally, he had to carry these heavy components on a sort of pannier over the front wheel of his bike. I told him to leave them at the post office and I would collect them (it was only 1½ miles away). His reply was that they were not allowed to do that. I bet he wished he had a white van and not a red bike.

***

There was a time when everything was delivered to the farms. People didn't do a big shop because there weren't the cars about then and they didn't or couldn't carry the shopping home. My mother used to get daily visits from the milkman and baker and weekly visits from the grocer and butcher. All that stopped when there were more cars about and with the advent of the supermarket.

Now we are back with deliveries again and life goes full circle, it always does. We rarely support the village community shop, I will tell you why sometime, and we are often frowned upon because of that. But the people who do the frowning often have the supermarket delivery van outside their house and we never do.

The dogs take great interest in white vans. They seem to regard them as public enemy number one. There are two farm dogs that make a great noise if there is a white van about and

Gomer hears them and insists on joining in. He wants to be let out and let back in so often that we have idly considered fitting a cat flap for him. But he is now too fat for any cat flap that I have ever seen. The dogs have never bitten anyone but they encourage each other to do so and for a stranger who doesn't know that they don't bite, they are a daunting sight. A white van comes this morning and the driver tells me that if I don't shut the dogs in, he won't come again. This proposed sanction does not have the effect he expected. I smile. Dogs could be the answer. I've got nothing against white van drivers, I often try to engage conversation or offer them a cup of tea but they have such a busy schedule they don't have time for either. Now some of them have started turning their vans on my lawn, bring on the dogs, I don't reckon much to that.

***

About a mile away, across the fields, is a big country house. If I describe it as a stately home you will get a better idea of what I mean. There are two big lakes in front of this house. These lakes used to be home to large numbers of Canada geese. There aren't so many now. There are reckoned to be over 70 swans there, I don't know who has counted them, but that's what they reckon. The fields in-between where I live and the lakes are low lying, (not my fields) and the swans scatter over these fields every spring. There are lots of depressions in these fields and they all fill with water in the winter. The swans, in their pairs, seek these bits of water out, set up home there and build nests. They are often disappointed because lots of these bits of water dry up as March turns into April. Some of these swans could be mine because my wife loves swans and over the years I have bought several swans from rescue centres for her and put them on our pond. They have always legged it to the lakes. The only swans she has on the pond now are two plastic ones and they are not likely to leg it anywhere. They are very life-like and I have even seen foxes looking at them and licking their lips.

There are probably twenty pairs of swans scattered over these fields and it's nice to see them. Not quite as nice when one brings the electric cables down and we have a power cut for about six hours on a late Sunday afternoon. Not so nice for the swan whose lifeless body was to be seen on the grass. For me there were pluses and minuses. On the upside I didn't have to watch any more of a Manchester United game; the downside was that I had to have sandwiches for my Sunday dinner.

10 April 2021

As we see the prospect of lockdown easing, as it slowly relinquishes the stranglehold it has over our lives, it gives us time to reflect on what has gone on thus far. I haven't missed going to the pub as much as I thought I would. I certainly haven't missed going to the cash point so often. What I have really missed is people calling by. We would get callers most days. They would sit around the kitchen table and talk, mostly about other people and farming. People often refer to this sort of chat as gossip. And they would be right.

***

The feral goats of Llandudno have made it onto the national news. Historically these goats have lived on a vast promontory called the Great Orme that borders the sea and the town. Now large numbers of them have found their way into the town where they lie about the streets as if they own the place, which they apparently do. Those that are tasked with looking after the goats, (unsuccessfully it would seem) say that the increase in numbers is due to the fact that last year they were not able to administer a contraception injection because of lockdown. They seem unconcerned that these goats will be a hazard to road users. Their short-term answer is that most of the straying goats are male and they will return to their traditional home when the next rut starts. That, by my reckoning, has to be about six months away. What will happen in the meantime and what will stop them returning? I suspect that, much like urban foxes, these goats have found that living in a town is easier than living on a windswept mountain. There is plenty to eat in gardens and on grassy verges and there is ample shelter from the wind behind walls and buildings.

If it was up to me, I would cull some or the problem will never go away and that is what they would do in most countries of the world. But, as a nation we have a strange attitude to culling. Cull some species and there is an outcry yet cull others in their thousands and no one says a word. If culling these goats is an unmentionable option, why not catch some and put them elsewhere?

Why do people invariably want to rewild with predator species? Why do they want to rewild with animals like the lynx when a few white billy goats are just as photogenic? Some people are advocating the reintroduction of wolves, which defies belief. What was the human population of this country when the last wolf was seen? Some people are strenuous protectors of a dangerous, destructive and unattractive animal like the wild boar, where does that come from? 'I like to see wild boar about, the rascals have been into Grandad's grave, but that's ok.' I volunteer to start re-homing some of those goats. I would put two nannies and one billy in the garden of 10 Downing Street. There is an enthusiastic rewilder lives nearby.

**

There was a time in my life when I was away from home on business a lot. I used to stay often in hotels. This is not the treat it sometimes seems. There was one hotel I used to use quite a lot. They knew me and I knew them. I booked in there late one afternoon. 'We are very busy Mr Evans and I'm sorry I have had to put you in the annexe.' 'That's ok.' 'I'll take you there.' 'There's no need, I'm sure I will find it.' But she insisted and I remember thinking that she seemed a bit agitated. Eventually we get to the room which is fine. And then she tells me she has another apology. 'This is the only room we have that doesn't have its own en-suite, but not to worry, this door opposite yours is your bathroom and no one else uses it, and we have left you a dressing gown to use as well.' And she is off.

None of this is a problem. In fact I am quite taken with the dressing gown. It is one of those white towelling ones with a hood, I have always thought they were cool. I have only ever had one dressing gown, quite smart, in a paisley pattern, it was given to me by my grandfather when I was 21! I wore it about four years later when I had my appendix out and that is the only time I wore it. It has been to hospital several times because various people have borrowed it.

I am very taken with the hotel dressing gown. It's the sort you would wear if you were a boxer and making your way to the ring for a title fight, a fantasy I have often enjoyed. Or you might wear it if you were in the Ku Klux Klan, I don't know where that thought came from, hoods and white robes I expect, which has never been a fantasy of mine!

Then I decide to have a shower. I don't need a shower, I had one at midday before I left home. I just want to use the towelling dressing gown. I get undressed and put the dressing gown on. It is soaking wet inside, clearly a previous occupant of the room has used it to have shower and then put it back on the hanger. It is cold and wet inside and felt horrible. It came off in very quick time. I often think of it and remember how it made me shudder. I didn't complain, I rarely do.

17 APRIL 2021

Talking of dressing gowns: the only house you can see out of our windows is another farmhouse and that is a mile away, and they don't have any windows pointing in our direction. Over the years I have got into the habit of wandering from bedroom to bathroom and back again without any clothes one, not a pretty sight, but I cannot do anything about that. Here is another hotel story. I was staying in a small hotel in London and went for a shower. My room was on the first floor, there was a bus-stop outside and the pavement was narrow. After my shower I wandered back into the bedroom completely nude. There was a bus stopped outside. The passengers on the top deck were about five yards away. I stared at them and they stared at me. I can just remember those that had seen me nudging those that had not and drawing their attention to me. Then the bus moved off and they probably never saw me again: that should not be an issue, there was not any more to see.

***

We go down to see my daughter every Sunday morning and yesterday we were talking about people who know nothing of farming but who assume that they do. Of whom there are plenty. A friend of mine is sitting in his armchair one Sunday afternoon, before he goes out to feed his cattle, when there is a sharp rap on his backdoor. So when he opens the door he is confronted by about ten people, who by the way they were dressed he takes to be ramblers. I use the word 'confronted' quite deliberately because he can tell right away that they are aggressive. They have an aggressive spokesman, a sort of Sergeant in the rambler army. 'Are those your sheep on that hill?' No 'Hello' or 'sorry to disturb you.' You can see his sheep and his hill from his backdoor. 'Yes.' 'They are so hungry they are eating rocks.' There are cries from the other ramblers of 'It's a disgrace.' And 'You should be ashamed.' My friend is at something of a loss, he has gone, in a very few minutes from sitting warm and content in his armchair to being accused of animal cruelty. His main concern is just why they should think his sheep are eating rocks.

Then he realises what the problem could be. The previous week he had taken a lot of Himalayan rock salt licks up on the hill for the sheep. This rock salt comes in big pink lumps, some are like boulders. They are much loved by sheep and cattle, who will lick them for hours. He explains all this to the ramblers and he can tell they don't believe him. So he puts his wellies on and takes them up the yard to see the rest of the delivery. They accept his explanation but he can tell they are not best pleased. They would much rather have found a case of animal cruelty. This is almost quite funny, but then it isn't. It is not funny that there are people about, who know so much about farming that they think that sheep eat rocks. These same people, or their organisations, will lobby politicians as to the future of the British countryside. Not that they know anything about what goes on in the countryside, not that they would see that that matters. These people had walked over a mile out of their way to complain about something that turned out to be completely wrong, just as wrong as it could be. That is very scary.

Then my daughter reminds me of another story. She used to be on the PTA of our village school. The school wanted to have a fundraising garden party, a sort of fete, and we said they could hold it here. The lady who was chair at the time wanted to come out and see if it was suitable. She had only lived in the countryside about three years. That does not matter but it's relevant to the story. She approves of it and they bring her out a cup of tea. I am mowing the lawn and I am asked to join them, I remember this clearly as it is the only time I have been given a cup of tea when I'm mowing the lawn.

So we are sitting down and our lady visitor is monopolising the conversation. 'I don't like dairy farming because the farmers, (guess she means me), keep their cows locked in sheds all the year round and they never feel the sun on their backs or get to walk on grass.' It is ironic that she should say this now, because it's a beautiful spring day and about twenty yards behind her the cows were coming in for afternoon milking. I could not resist this, 'How did they get out?' She looks over her shoulder and sees the cows. 'Look how contented they are, I told you they prefer to be out.' I didn't say anything, I didn't need to. When she first arrived and was doing her inspection, there were over 100 cows lying out in the sun about 400 yards away. She did not see them because she didn't want to. She had a preconceived idea and she wasn't about to have it spoiled. People only see what they want to see.

21 April 2021

I know April is supposed to be a spring month, but where we live it can still send along some winter. The grass is growing, just, and the cows are out night and day, always a good thing for man and beast. They go off to their grazing after every milking, down their track, but it is a journey of optimism rather than of fulfilment and we are still having to give them a lot of silage.

But I have been able to get some advantage out of the spring. The ground has dried up and the fields we use for silage do not yet have much grass on them so I can drive around where I like. I have been assessing the numbers of hares. Now that the evenings are lighter I even drove after tea, and parked under a tree for an hour. In a month I have seen just one hare. Our tractor driver, who is often up there all day, reckons there are eight or nine. Five years ago there could be that number in every field. The keeper reckoned there were over a hundred up there then. At this time of year they were so preoccupied with making more hares that you could drive right up to them and they would carry on with their chasing and boxing as if you didn't exist. They would chase each other around the trunk for ages and then, for some reason that I could never detect, they would all leg it but often only as far as the next field. The activities of the hare coursers has taken its toll. They kill lots of big hares in the autumn. The buzzards and red kites take lots of leverets in the spring. Seems we cannot do much about either. I know of some estates and farms where they focussed on the trespass of coursers rather than the fate of the hares. It did not take them long to work out that if they didn't have hares, then the coursers wouldn't come. So they shot all the hares. Sad but true.

***

I never thought I would see the day, but there you are, a bar has appeared in our garden. My grandsons have built one out of pallets, it's quite tidy, not the eyesore I expected. I think the driving principal was, 'the pubs are closed so let's build our own.' The bar is open most nights and is often preceded by two or three-a-side football; they have bought some goalposts. Some nights there is a barbeque for about six people. I have noticed that their various guests never come empty handed and always bring bottles, cans and food.

It's quite sophisticated because once it was built they added refinements. There is a clock on the wall behind the bar, which doesn't work and there is also a refrigerator, which they bought on Facebook, which does. I've been a couple of times and have noticed that our garden furniture it getting worse for wear. Especially the table, which is best described as lots of holes held up by some legs. When we first bought it we used to put it in the dry every winter but the best of intentions can fall by the wayside.

Now here is an interesting thing. These boys are at the age when it is customary to have a glass in their hand. But they noticed that it is so much cheaper to buy their drink in the supermarket than the pub that they are starting to question if they need the pub. I wonder how many others will now feel the same way and if that thinking will accelerate the demise of the pub? Me, I am not bothered about drinking at home but prefer to sit at the pub and listen to the chat. Bet they go back to the pub when the nights get darker and it starts to get cold. But I get a lot of pleasure from the fact that although there is a two generation gap, these boys are quite happy to mix with us and introduce us to their friends. No need to tell them that, though.

***

One of the downsides of having a big house, apart from the cold, is that people think it will be a good venue for fundraising activity. Over the years we have gladly allowed people to use our house in this way. It was mostly for the village school, with which I was involved for many years. The secret of a good fundraiser is that people are allowed a good time and then they will come again. We used to have functions for the school that were supposed to finish at 10.30. There would often be people here at 2 or 3 o'clock in the morning. I used to wear nightshirts then and remember one year I went upstairs and put one on and made myself some cocoa before those that were still in the kitchen took the hint. If you have to be up before five to milk it tends to focus your mind.

We once had a cheese and wine here for the rugby club. The main fundraiser was supposed to be at a tombola but unfortunately we had some donkeys at the time. They fetched one in the house and made a lot of money charging 50p for a ride. Ladies with their tight skirts on were free. That is probably sexist now but it wasn't then. You are probably not allowed to write that now, let alone think it. I get the clear impression that those of us in the silent majority are getting a bit fed up with being told what we can write or say.

***

This friend of mine is in the garden centre. He is approached by another customer who is carrying an aerosol can of insecticide. 'Can you tell me if this is any good for wasps?' 'It's no good at all, it will kill them.'

1 MAY 2021

It would be quite difficult for me to describe the commitment that goes into being a dairy farmer. For example, I milked cows on Christmas Day for over 50 years. I cannot do it now, my knees can't do it, but I wish I could. I did not have to do it, I chose to do it, and I would choose to do it again. It's not a unique phenomenon, lots of dairy farmers have done the same. I never felt hard done by doing it, but I used to get mildly irritated when friends who worked in other industries used to ask me how much time I had off for Christmas. They often had from the 23rd December until the 2nd January off. It wasn't taken out of their annual leave, they just had it off. I was not irritated by envy, it just used to irritate me that although they lived in a rural area, they had no concept of how dairy farming was a seven day a week job.

I know of dairy farmers whose children are grown up now but who have never had a holiday with them, not even one day on a beach. It is a fact of life that on small family dairy farms there might only be the farmer and his wife who could do the milking, so organising family holidays was very difficult. Organising a relief milker was often difficult and expensive, so it was easier and less hassle to stay at home. This happens less often now because herds are bigger and there are more people who can milk on each farm.

Being a farmer can be a fulfilling life and some people have never felt the need for a holiday. I have a friend who comes into this category. When my parents were elderly they had a holiday in Torquay so I went to fetch them back. I told my friend and he had never been to Torquay so he came down for the ride. After we dropped my parents off I suggested that we go a different way home so he could see some 'new' country. He declined this as he wanted to get home to go around his sheep and cattle. He is a man who never ever goes on holiday but I don't know of anyone who is more content. Who is to say that he has not got life right, all along.

***

I was talking about commitment, but I digressed. There was a photograph in my weekly farming magazine. It was of a dairy farm in Australia in the area recently affected by floods. Without going into the technicalities of milking parlour design, it was what we call a herringbone parlour. The cows walk in on ground level and the operator works in a pit in the middle, so the cows udders are at his eye level. Except that the cows were paddling in about a foot of water, which put their udders just above the water level. The poor farmer was in the pit, up to his chest in water, trying to milk them. The milk would be of no value, the whole milking exercise would be driven by the welfare needs of emptying the cows' full udders. My practical dairy farmer's head is full of ideas. How would they get power to the vacuum pump which is also likely to be underwater? I have never milked cows up to my chest in water. I have never had to show that sort of commitment. And besides, if you are in Australia, you never know what might be in the water anyway.

***

The cycle of sheep is an important part of the farming calendar. If we start in the autumn, we were then buying new ewes and rams. All was quiet then until after Christmas when the ewes were scanned to see how many lambs they were carrying. If someone had a particularly good scan they would brag about it in the pub. When I used to keep ewes and I had them scanned, I never told anyone how we had got on. Too much counting your chicken before they are hatched about it for my liking.

One year a farmer was so pleased with his scanning that he quietly showed me a scrap of paper with the scanning results on. He was a farmer with a lot of sheep, probably thousands but no one knew exactly how many. I was not interested in the scanning results. I was adding up how many ewes he had. I was nearly finished when he realised what I was doing and he snatched the paper back.

They were strangely quiet this year about scanning results. Now there are ewes and all the new-born lambs in the fields.

But a part of the story is missing. Because of covid restrictions we have not heard anything of the actual lambing. Lambing stories tend to be either of triumph or disaster. It's no good relating the mundane such as, 'I had a ewe have twins yesterday.' Everyone has got a ewe who had twins. No, what will grab your attention is if a ewe had four or five lambs. I had ewes that had this number lots of times. It IS a problem that you get when you lamb indoors. A ewe very close to lambing will steal lambs off a ewe that has already lambed, it is called mismothering, so by the time she has lambed her own lambs, she can have a large litter of lambs about her. It can take ages to sort out which lamb goes with which ewe.

You cannot beat someone being present at lambing all the time, but if you are on your own and you sneak back into the house for an hour in the warm on the settee and that hour turns into two hours and you get back into he shed and there is a case of mismothering to sort out, you have all day for regrets. Sometimes someone will say that they have lost several lambs because of bad lambings. I would never say anything except an inward 'phew', they lost more than me. The time for this year's lambing stories is gone now and we will probably never hear them, but not to worry. It will soon be time for shearing.

8 May 2021

My daughter works for the NHS. She isn't a nurse, she looks at people's eyes. As do I, but that is another story. Nevertheless she has found the last 12 months to be hard work, not least because she suffers from asthma and she has had to wear all the protective kit. Every year she takes two weeks annual leave so she can help with the lambing. She has two big problems in her life: she has me for a father and she follows social media. (I don't ever have a problem with social media because I never look at it).

One of the most useful tools you have when you are lambing are cans of aerosol paint spray marker which you use to identify ewes and lambs. For example, when I kept sheep I might spray a ewe with red 27 and her lambs likewise, so then I would make a note in a little book, 27+2, and I would know that ewe number 27 had two lambs. If I had a question mark in my mind about a ewe, for example, if she had had a hard lambing or if I wasn't sure about her milk supply, I would use a blue mark then I could give them special attention when they were outside at grass.

The thing about some sheep is that they are only happy when they are trying to die and they are at their happiest when they are dead. However many ewes you have and whatever your system at lambing, it is all designed to keep ewe and lambs alive and well. Some ewes, by their behaviour, will challenge your system. My daughter is looking on social media and she reads an account by a sheep farmer who had a ewe that had given him such a hard time that he had written a derogatory word on her side with spray paint. A sort of graffiti on wool. All my daughter had replied was that she wished she had thought of doing that because a ewe had knocked her down that morning when she was trying to catch it. This attracted the attention of a vegan troll who said that she wished she had been there to knock her down as well. My daughter found this to be quite upsetting. I know I often tease vegans and probably wind them up, but I never wish them any harm. But my daughter tells me she got off lightly; she says that there are some awful things on social media. She read me one where a vegan had wished a farmer's wife and her young children were dead. There are some nasty people out there.

***

I've got this friend who lives not far away. He is a superb gardener. At the bottom of his garden is a pig sty. He used to keep two pigs there every year. That is how traditional country gardens used to work. The pigs used to eat all the scrap from the house and all the waste from the garden and the manure from the pigs would grow the vegetables next year. I won't say what happened to the pigs in case I get trolled but I will just say that in days past the pigs were an important part of a family's diet. He is very generous to us and in late summer and the autumn he gives us lots of his surplus produce. But best of all, I have a weakness for fried tomatoes and he brings us loads of tomatoes. It's not all one-way, because in return I let him catch the moles in our lawn.

When he stopped keeping pigs I used to take him some farmyard manure every year. Now I don't have to take him any, he's found another source of manure. There's a small family circus based in our village. It's always been there, their children used to go to school with our children. It was a common sight to see a bear sitting in the front seat of a Land Rover with a seat belt around him. Years ago I took my youngest grandchildren to see the circus and they were fascinated. The man who took your money was likely to be the ring master.

I know that a circus is not everyone's idea of fun but this was run by that local family. And I think I do know a bit about animals, so I particularly looked out for any animals that looked stressed. I didn't see one, they all looked well cared for and content. The only animal that didn't look as if it wasn't enjoying itself was the fox that was riding the Shetland pony around the ring. That might have been because the local hunt kennels were only two fields away.

But there are implications. My friend now gets his manure from the circus. He tells me that the cabbage will be grown with zebra manure, the beans with camel and the tomatoes with monkey poo. Not sure I fancy the tomatoes. Will need to think about that.

15 May 2021

I remember that once my son took his boys skating. During their outing he fell down and broke his ankle. There were two incidents that he reported. Firstly he reckoned that the management had him sign a disclaimer that it was his own fault almost before he hit the ice. And when he was in the ambulance the paramedic asked him if he wanted oxygen to relieve the pain. He said no. The attendant said that there were only two sorts of people who said no to oxygen, farmers and rugby players. My son told him he was both. Men have quite a cavalier attitude to their own health, I know, I am supposed to take some pills every day but I am always forgetting. I rarely go to the doctors, it always seems like a good place to catch something. I remember going once and sitting in the waiting room and opposite me were two farmers that I knew had cancer. I felt a complete fraud. They didn't live long after. I can't remember why I was there but it was very trivial in comparison.

***

The reluctance of men to go to the doctors is well chronicled. The last time I saw my doctor was when he was walking a footpath over my fields so I don't think that really counts. If you ask him anything medical whilst he is off duty, he tells you to google it, which is fair enough. My son started playing rugby for our club when he was 15 and we played in the same team for three years. If either of us got injured we always went to the vets first for an x-ray. If it was difficult to diagnose we then took the x-ray to the doctors. It was so much quicker than going to A&E. Often all the injuries wanted was time and as long as we could play the next Saturday, that was all that mattered. My son used to pick up lots of cuts to his head and always had them stitched up by the vet. He could shower after a game, go to Saturday evening surgery at the vets, get stitched up and be back in bar in an hour and a half. People with dogs and cats would let him jump the queue. I used to take the stitches out. I never charged him but neither did the vet for putting them in.

***

A few years ago I had to have an operation on one of my knees. It was no big job, not worth making a fuss. I had to have general anaesthetic but I didn't have to stay overnight. They put me in a ward to get me ready, there were about ten men in there who had all had new knees. Half of them were dairy farmers and I knew most of them. About a month later I'm in a bar in Cardiff before an international rugby match. A group of farmers, who I know very well, comes in, and with them is the surgeon who did my knee. I don't pretend that he is a friend, just that I know him by sight. Anyway we get talking and he asks how my knee is. I say ok and then I say, 'I've got an appointment to see you next Wednesday.' He says, 'What's that for?' and I tell him that it's for a post op check up. So he sits me down, rolls my trouser leg up and thoroughly examines my knee. 'There that's fine, there's no need for you to come next Wednesday.' That's always stuck in my mind as a proper bit of doctoring. It saved me a round trip of 70 miles and half a day as well.

***

My daughter looks after me more than my doctor. She takes my blood pressure regularly, about every two years, she cuts my hair. She nags me if I need nagging. She always has my back. All this is fair enough because she took a lot of looking after as a baby. As a baby she was hyperactive, which is a kindly way to describe it. We used to put her in her cot at about 10pm but by two in the morning she was ready to get up. She would stand in her cot and bounce it around the room. She was making such an impact on our lives that my wife and I made a deal. She would look after her in the early hours but I would take her downstairs at 5am when I got up.

We had a lad working here at the time who could do the morning milking so I spent the time in our kitchen listening to radio four and drinking tea. My daughter would be crawling around the kitchen trying to wreck it. That scenario was ok when it was dark in the mornings but when it got lighter I wanted to be outside and doing some work.

So I used to put my daughter in a bucket and take her with me. I thought this to be quite handy as I could put her down anywhere and keep her clean. She still couldn't walk then and she soon found out that if I left her and her bucket unattended, she could rock it until it fell onto its side and then she could crawl off in the mud. The bucket was too tall for her to climb out of so if I wanted to leave her anywhere I hit on the idea of putting the handle over a gate hinge.

Once I started doing that I was back in control. I could leave her somewhere safely and return to the feed store and fetch some feed for pigs or calves. She was good as gold when she was in her bucket, she used to watch what was going on, her little hands grasping the lid of the bucket and her eyes just peering over the top.

22 May 2021

At this time of year we pay a lot of attention to our pond. In the middle of the pond is a tiny island and every year a Canada goose builds a nest there and it is always interesting to see how many young she will hatch out. She is later than usual this year, I wonder if it's because of the cold weather? Our pond always gets a lot of interest from the local Canada geese who see it as a potential nest site. But the island is only big enough for one nest. This year she has hatched five out but two days later there are seven. I think that another goose has hatched two elsewhere and brought them to the pond. If I am right it means our pond has become a sort of Canada goose creche. We have an acre and a half of wood with a stream running though it but that is about 300 yards away and 300 yards is a long way for a young gosling to walk. On our pond we also have two plastic swans although they have never bred, which is a bit of a disappointment.

But I am not the only one watching the pond. All the local winged predators are watching as well. First amongst them are the red kites. They fly slowly over the goslings, seemingly all day long, looking for a chance of an easy meal. In the immediate background are the buzzards and then the carrion crows. We had this creche phenomenon last year and then there were ten goslings but they had all disappeared within a week.

There is a sort of pecking order, perhaps pecking order is the wrong phrase, perhaps I should use the word, hierarchy, to these ariel predators. The red kites are clearly the boss, they are first in the queue. They come before the buzzards who in turn come before the carrion crows. It's not that we think Canada geese are special but we like to see them about as they grow and as if at some signal they all fly off to the lakes about a mile away where the parents came from all along. We know that the kites and buzzards are only doing what comes naturally to them but we also feel that they are our goslings on our pond and we feel protective to them. I often wonder if people will ever realise what damage these predator birds do. Probably not.

***

When you are a farmer you expect things to go wrong. In fact your ability to cope with things that go wrong is often a measure of how good you are as a farmer. Things that go wrong should be viewed as a challenge and should be treated as such. You should spend your energy on overcoming the challenge and not let it wind you up. Thus when I came into our kitchen one Saturday morning and found it to be flooded by about half an inch of water, I didn't panic. My first thought was to identify what the problem was. It was the feed to our washing machine.

My second thought was that as it was a Saturday it might be next week before we could get a plumber. Most people would say that all we had to do was turn the water off. Oh, that life was that simple!

This farm was always very short of water, until the mains water came. On the day before we went on mains water, there were churns of water in the kitchen to wash dishes and cook with. We were carrying buckets of water upstairs to flush toilets. There were churns of water in the dairy to wash the milking equipment and we had a tanker of river water to wash the milking parlour out.

So when we put the mains in, we linked it straight from the house to the farm which means it is not an option to turn the water off because you would cut off the water to the farm at the same time.

When my wife sees the flood in the kitchen she opens the door and sweeps some outside. Then she asks why we can't turn it off. I explain, very much as I've explained to you. Then she asks how long do I think it will be before we can get it fixed. I think that in a marriage it's important not to give false hopes, so I say three months. I don't think for a minute it will take that long but you have to start somewhere. 'You have to be joking, I'm not going to paddle around in this for three months.' 'I'll put some stepping stones in.' On Monday I manage to get the plumber – he says he is in the middle of a big job that he can't leave but he will come on Tuesday. The leak is getting worse but now I know it will only be another 24 hours. So I decide that I can safely wind my wife up a bit more; she is getting very tetchy about the situation. She always goes shopping on Mondays and she always asks me if I want anything. I say I could do with half a dozen goldfish. 'Whatever do you want some goldfish for?' 'I thought they could swim about the kitchen, I thought they would make a nice feature.' I won't tell you what she said.

The plumber came when he said, he fixed it in an hour, we swept out the last of the water, left the door open to dry the floor. And in another hour you couldn't tell there had ever been a flood.

29 May 2021

Last year our landlord had to take down some fences so that he could extract some timber from his woods. We graze the fields adjacent with dry cows and heifers and we could control them with temporary electric fences. But the landlord has not yet reinstated the fences and our electric fences won't do any more. Every morning there are five deer in the fields. Deer are no respecters of electric fences. We are concerned that they will knock the fences down in the night and that the cows will get into the woods and damage the newly planted trees. The deer will probably do the same, but they are not my deer!

More of a problem are the deer that appear on the fields at home where we try to organise a stricter grazing regime for the milking cows. There are 15 deer there every morning and they fetch so many electric fences down every night that there is a real chance that they will compromise the whole grazing system.

It's very strange because ten years ago we would see about one deer a year and now we see deer every day. It was so rare that you would tell people about it. Deer are free spirits, they can go where they like and eat what they will. Conventional fences and hedges that divide farmland are no barrier to them.

A farmer I know used to grow a field of swedes every year. He used to put his ewes on there every year after Christmas and the swedes would keep the sheep until they started to lamb at the end of March. His farm is surrounded by woods and every night 50 deer would come out of the woods to eat the swedes. It got so bad that the last year he did it, the swedes only lasted a couple of weeks into February and then they were all gone. He tried to stop the deer getting out of the woods by putting an electric fence above the conventional fence but that only worked for one night. The deer simply went down another field, along the road, and jumped the gate. They stopped this particular farmer growing swedes and he had to feed his ewes round bale silage but the deer still come for that!

I remember once going to speak at a dinner and staying the night at a farm. Next day the farmer took me for a ride to see his farm. This is compulsory if you stay on a farm. We were going along a track in his Land Rover, around a wood. We went around a sharp corner and there were two red deer hinds about twenty yards in front of us. They were grazing on the side of the track and obviously hadn't heard us coming. I shall never forget how they cleared the fence back into the wood. The fence was what we call pig netting, it's mostly put up to stop sheep, it was probably three to four feet high. The two deer were standing next to it and they just sprang over it. No run up, nothing, just as if they were on springs, over the fence and gone! That's why deer mostly look so well, they can go where they will and choose what to eat.

I see that there is a move to reintroduce wolves to Scotland. 'They' say that the wolves will control the numbers of deer. That is probably right, just until the wolves work out that sheep and old age pensioners are easier to catch than deer. I often fear just what lies ahead for the countryside in this country. My story about ramblers who thought sheep eat rocks should never be forgotten. They are the same people who think that wolves are a good idea.

***

I haven't been to the pub although it's been open. You have to drink outside there. I can't see the point of sitting there in the cold when I can get cold sitting at home without the expense. Those that have been tell me it gets very cold once the sun goes down even though they have built an outside covered area for drinkers and have outside heaters. 9 o'clock is enough for most people. One enterprising local landlady has gone on social media and advised potential customers to take a hot water bottle to put in to their laps and that she will replenish it with hot water during the evening.

***

My youngest grandson is 15 today but already he is looking forward to when he is 16. When he is 16 he says he will get a motorbike. I think he means a scooter. I sense that his immediate family are not keen but they have 12 months to persuade him otherwise. He is a sensible lad so I expect he will be ok. I don't say anything because I had a motorbike when I was 16. I took my test on it just so I could take a girl home from Young Farmers. I took her home once but she told her Dad and he forbade her to ride on it again. What a waste of time and effort that was. I sold the bike and bought my first car which cost me £25 and that was a big social step forward. Taking your test on a motorbike is quite an experience – the examiner walks about and watches you.

5 June 2021

Most people would have thought it would be the end to their life, as they know it. I've just spent a week without a mobile phone and laptop. This experience has taught me that the phone is more important in my life than the laptop, by some distance. It isn't a smart phone. All I need of a phone is to make and receive calls and texts, I don't need anything else. The mobile phone is very useful for a farmer, it can summon help if something should go wrong, and something going wrong can be a daily occurrence. Things like a puncture in a tractor a mile or so from home or stock straying when someone has left a gate open. It turned out that there was nothing wrong with the phone, it was the charger that was at fault. So it took me a week to work that out. I dread the day that my phone should die and I can't get a simple old fashioned, push-button replacement without a touch screen.

I had to have a new phone about three months ago and the contact list did not transfer, which is a big nuisance. I'm putting the names in now, but there are still a lot missing. Last week I had two texts that were very similar in content. 'Now that lockdown is easing and as we are in your area I thought we would call in.' I replied the same to both. 'It will be good to see you, please do.' I didn't have a clue who they were from but I wasn't about to say so.

I occasionally wonder what happened to my first mobile phone. It was one that was the size of a house brick with an aerial sticking out, I know that I didn't throw it away but where it is now is a mystery. I've always looked at my laptop twice a day at the same times so at first I missed the routine. Broadband is very slow around here. You can compose an email and when you try to put a full stop at the end, then you have time to make a cup of tea before the full stop appears on your screen. I don't pretend to any IT competence, I can send emails and reply to them, but if anything goes wrong it's then I struggle. If there are no grandchildren about then I struggle a bit longer, that's why it was out of action for a week. At first I missed my laptop, I missed the regular discipline of looking at it twice a day but when it was back, looking at it was a chore. I was still alive and well and the important things in life continued anyway. The weather was awful and cows still calved. I started to wonder if I needed an online presence at all. If someone had an urgent message they could always call me on my mobile phone or drop by. Most days I get about 12 emails, ten of these are either selling something or promoting something. Do I need that amount of intrusion in my life? No I don't.

***

They are having elections in Scotland. My work used to take me to Scotland a lot. I have a lot of friends in Scotland and don't now see them as often as I'd like. Looking back, there are three things that stick in my mind. Firstly, I couldn't get over the difference in daylight hours. It's not that far north, in the great scheme of things, but it was still dark in the mornings at 9 o'clock in the winter, and in the summer, there was always an extra hour of daylight compared with what we had at home!

Secondly, if you were going to meet someone they would always say, 'I'll be there at the back of 2 o'clock.' I asked for them to explain this several times but I never knew what they meant. Did they mean just before two or just after? It was a mystery to me. I can't do with being late so I always used to opt for 'just before'. Thirdly, and probably the most amusing, they had a saying, 'she's a nippy sweetie.' It was always applied to a small feisty woman who had plenty to say and wasn't afraid to say it. If she thought you deserved the sharp edge of her tongue, that's what you would get. If we are talking about Scottish elections, and we were, does that remind you of anyone?

12 JUNE 2021

There are lots of things in life I don't understand and one of them is social media. Most people would hail it as the success story of the age but I would see it as the opposite. Not a day goes by when you don't hear or read of someone who has suffered abuse in some way on social media. Some of this abuse is so bad I find it difficult to understand why anyone would feel the need to say such horrific things. They only do it because they can do it anonymously. If I meet someone I don't like, I don't bother with them. I can't remember ever hating anyone, in fact even with people I don't like there is usually a part of them that is ok.

Sometime last year there was a little boy here, I think he was six. He came to sit by me as I was writing and he said 'Are you on Facebook?' I said I wasn't so he put me on. It was noted by the ladies in the pub on the Saturday night, 'Roger's on Facebook.' I have never looked at it or used it.

There is a widespread view that the companies which own social media should police the hate content but I think that will never happen. It's much too big now and that particular horse is well out of the stable. But there is a very simple answer. If people say nasty things about you on social media and it upsets you, why do you look? I like it if people like me, I am sure that most people are the same. If someone dislikes you or even hates you on social media, let them get on with it, you don't have to give them the satisfaction of knowing you have read it. Take back control, it's easily done, they get their satisfaction from their anonymity and the distress they cause. If the distress disappears perhaps the hate will as well.

***

Politicians have an annoying habit of using the 'green' word at every chance they get. They just love to say 'green'. They know that it will win votes and that if they say it often enough, voters will think it's an important part of their agenda. And then they say that it will be a good thing to bring food all the way from Australia. What's green about that?

There are negatives to Australian food. They have droughts there and floods and bushfires so sometimes the food will not turn up and what then? The animals are kept in such vast numbers that health and management are administered on a herd or flock basis. It is inevitable that some animals don't get treated. These animals often live in a harsh, competitive environment and for a percentage, staying alive is a real challenge. Yesterday, on my ride around, I met ten ramblers. They were walking through my cattle. If one of those cattle wasn't well, I'm sure the RSPCA would soon know. There's no such public scrutiny in Australia. I once met a farmer who had spent a week on a huge sheep and cattle station. What he told me that goes on there is too awful to repeat.

**

Yesterday I was on my daily ride around my fields. These fields are earmarked to be cut for silage but as yet there is not much growth on them. I can see two hares lying fairly close together in the grass so I drive towards them. The two hares break cover and lope unhurriedly away. Five years ago if I hadn't seen ten hares by now I would wonder where they all are. But we are where we are, and these two hares tell me quite a lot. They are only half grown so they are clearly this year's 'hatch'. They are identical in size so they could be twins, and they are staying close together. If a hare had reared twins with so many winged predators about ,that can only be a good thing. It also tell me that if these are young half-grown hares, there must be two more hares about somewhere, the Dad and Mum.

Our journey takes us the same way as the hares are running but they keep about thirty yards in front. The dog Gomer whimpers in delight. He would love to be let out to chase them but they won't be chased until the coursers come in the autumn. Hare coursing was alluded to in the Queen's speech when she opened parliament, so perhaps the end of illegal coursing is in sight. We move on to the next field and leave the hares picking at the clover. Gomer gives a sigh of disappointment.

It's the Eurovision Song Contest tonight. I'll probably pass on that but there is one I remember. When I left school I went to work on a farm where I lived in 'as family'. One mid-week they had their first TV set. It was a bit of a novelty and on the Saturday night we all sat down in a semi-circle to watch the Eurovision Song Contest. It was all very interesting until we got to the voting. The farmer's in-laws lived there as well and the granny got quite indignant because 'we' weren't doing very well. In the end she exploded, 'This is ridiculous, all those other were singing in foreign, I couldn't understand a word they were saying.'

19 JUNE 2021

Right in the middle of a 25 acre field that we have shut up for silage is a fallow deer hind and she has a fawn with her. When they are lying down in the grass you can hardly see them. They are quite safe, you have to be in the field to know they are there. Everything they are likely to need is close at hand. There is no water but I suspect that the wet grass provides most of the moisture they need. They don't move far and you can see where they have grazed. If I were a deer I would move in with them because they have chosen an idyllic spot. Some farmers would be agonised about how much grass they were eating but this farmer is quite pleased to see them. Lucky me.

When I get up on the Saturday morning of the Bank Holiday weekend, there is a motorbike parked outside our kitchen lawn. Nothing my grandsons do surprises me anymore and I just assume that they have invited a college friend to stay for the weekend. The only reservations I have is that I have never heard them mention a friend who has a motorbike. It is a part of my plan to mow the lawns today but I am well on top of them, so a day or two won't matter. We don't see anyone all day to confirm our assumptions but at 6 o'clock the motorbike and tent are still there.

We have booked ourselves in the for a bar meal at the pub. Neither of us has been there for months and we believe in the maxim, 'Use it or lose it'. We go early because Ann wants to get home to watch a football match on TV. A part of her wants to see Man City win but a bigger part wants to see Chelsea lose, I don't know what Chelsea have ever done to her but there you are.

The pub is very busy, it has its own campsite but that is full and they have to move tents and caravans to the next field. We are in the dining room but we are close enough to the bar to talk to the regulars who are drinking in there. One of them shouts out, 'Did you two have your teeth checked out today?' He can see right away that we haven't a clue what he is talking about, so he tells us this story.

Apparently he was in the pub the previous evening, as was our son David. In keeping with covid rules, they all have to be sitting down but the tables are close enough so that they can all talk. The ladies who manage the pub come in with a complete stranger and they squeeze him in with the locals. They soon start to interrogate him. He is in the area for the first time and that he has booked into a course that teaches people how to ride motorbikes off road and in forestry but the course has been cancelled because the man who takes it is ill. He's come all the way from London and now is at a loss to know what to do. He also tells them that he is a dentist and would love to see a cow being milked. He can't realise that there is a good chance for him to see that because he is sitting next to my son.

When my son goes home he takes the dentist with him. That's why there is a motorbike outside our kitchen door and a tent in the middle of our lawn. When we go home at 8ish, our son has some cows close to calving in the field in front of our house. He is calving one of them and there is someone with him that we assume is the dentist. On the Sunday morning the tent comes down, is folded up and put on the bike. We get a cheery wave and he is off. When I see my son later he tells me that the dentist was in the parlour at a quarter to five on both mornings and worked with him all day. That's the story of when a dentist helped us with the milking. I never met him which is a pity, as I have a small filling that has come out.

26 JUNE 2021

Wool is a funny thing old thing. In medieval times it was associated with great wealth. There are fine buildings and churches built by the profit of the wool trade. Shearing used to be an important activity in the farming calendar but now it's just a chore. Shearing has been late this year, because it's been so cold and wool yields have been down because ewes have shed their belly wool. If you were shearing and had a ewe with a clear belly, well that would make your day. At one time there was so much money in wool it brought about the highland clearances and I can remember farmers telling me that it was used to pay the rent. When I kept sheep, the wool money used to pay for all the drenches and medicines. Now it doesn't even pay for the shearing.

***

A friend of mine has worked in the woods all his life. He was always been self employed, that's how work in the woods seems to function. There is a lot like him and they never seem short of something to do. Their work is seasonal: in autumn and winter they might be planting new trees; in spring and summer they might be clearing the undergrowth from around the trees they planted the previous year. On top of that there might be an area of trees that are ready to come down, mostly conifers, so they clear fell that but that clears an area that wants planting anew and so it goes on. Working in the woods used to be a big thing years ago but now, just like farming, a lot of work is mechanised when it used to be done by hand. A lot of softwood trees around here used to go to South Wales as pit props, not any more they don't. I can remember that when I first started farming they were thinning out a big larch wood next to my fields. They were using two horses to pull the trees out of the wood onto my fields. They asked if it was alright to let the horses graze on my fields at night. I said it was ok and the men who owned the horses said, 'How much?' I said it was free; I can still remember the puzzled look on their faces as they tried to work out if there was a catch in it.

***

I had a really good man who once worked for me (he is long gone now) but for twenty years he took a load of pit props to South Wales every day. He used to set off early each morning and he had to get back in time to put a load on for the next day. The only mechanisation they had available to them was the most basic of cranes, a sort of tripod. All this consisted of was a wire rope put through some pulleys. At one end they would put the wire around a bundle of pit props and the other was tied to a tractor. When the tractor reversed the load would rise up and they would drive the lorry under it. It doesn't sound much but freshly cut pit props are very heavy, especially if you have to lift them by hand.

One day as they were putting a load on, their boss turned up, he watched them for a while and then he said that they were not to use the crane for two weeks as it needed a rest! For good measure he took the key out of the tractor so that they couldn't use it. Bet he wouldn't get away with that today.

***

Anyway, back to my friend. He is asked to help plant a new wood. There are three of them involved in this work. One of them got the job so he is a sort of foreman and he takes life very seriously. It's quite a big job but they soon notice that rabbits are damaging the young trees they have planted. The leader is so concerned about this that he brings five snares to work on the Friday and puts them out on rabbit runs before he goes home. Sometimes over the weekend the other two go tickling trout. Poachers is an unkindly word so we won't use that. They catch quite a lot of trout and on the Sunday they take the five smallest to the wood where they are working and put them in the rabbit snares. On the Monday they go to continue planting trees and the foreman tells them to carry on whilst he goes around his rabbit wires. You can only imagine his reaction when he found the first fish. As I said, he takes life very seriously. And then he found another four. We will leave that story now because when he got back to his companions, the bad language was terrible. Knowing them as I do, I bet they lit a fire at about 12 o'clock and had trout for lunch. And I bet they had roast rabbit before the week was out.

3 JULY 2021

I am not good at looking at bits of paper, never have been. I only open the post about twice a week. I have always been of the opinion that the best place for a piece of paper is within the envelope it came in, and the best place for that envelope is on the pile of other envelopes that are stacked up by my place on the kitchen table. It is only when this pile gets top heavy and falls to the floor that I then open the envelopes. Most of our post is bills and I put them in a drawer but if it is more important than that, I put the piece of paper in a safe place. Trouble is I can never remember where that safe place is and that is why I seem to spend my life looking for it. Fortunately, help is at hand. We have a farm secretary who comes for half a day once a fortnight. She brings an order to it all. If she is coming I make an attempt to present her with the relevant post. If I don't get it right we get rolling eyes and deep sighs. I always remember when she is coming, it is the same day we put our black wheely bins out. Truth be told, I am a bit scared of her, but I wouldn't want her to know that. She gives the impression that her other clients are more organised and computer savvy than me, which isn't difficult to believe, but she has been coming here for over thirty years and is one of the family. So I've set the scene, here's the story.

***

I have a selective approach to bills. If there's the bill for twenty tons of cow cake in the pipeline I look for that, and work out how to pay for it. I particularly look out for any work done on a machine that has broken down, and no matter what you guess, it will always cost more. The big bills are all a part of my consciousness. The little bills less so. The secretary comes to me and says she has been looking at our landline telephone bill and she has found one call that has cost £80 and several for £50. She is so tenacious on these bills that she has my attention, do I mind if she phones the service provider? I think there must be a simple mistake, we hardly ever use the landline. I can hear her on the phone in the next room and I can tell by her voice that she is giving someone a hard time. I am almost starting to feel sorry for them.

We have all seen or heard on the media of people getting scammed out of money. We get a call most weeks from someone who says that if we don't send some money this morning we will be arrested this afternoon. We don't take any notice now but these calls must be really scary if you are elderly and living on your own. Eventually my secretary reports back, she was surely on the phone an hour. Seems we had been scammed after all. The expensive calls were made by someone in Salt Lake City in the States who had somehow got our phone number and was using it. Don't ask me how it works.

What was most worrying was the complete indifference of the service provider. They refused to take any action to block these calls, saying they would block them when they got to £200 a time. I won't pay their bill, that should get their attention.

After tea and when we are on with the silage I go to see how the workers are getting on. For years we have used contractors who did the whole job, they used to take about 12 hours and there were eight or nine men involved. This year we are doing it ourselves. The same man has to cut it, rake it and cart it but he always seems to do a field a day and it is much less frenetic.

So I arrive in the partially-cleared silage field and the first job is to let the dog out for a run. I know there is a hare down in this corner but she won't run far because she has twin leverets in the hedge. There she goes, the dog gives chase. When he wants to go top speed he puts his head down and looks over his shoulder to make sure I am watching. He doesn't get closer than ten yards away from the hare. The ten yards is of her choosing. The grass is raked up to be collected, twenty yards of grass in one swath. The hare can leap this in one bound, the dog can't.

I drive on and we see two more hares. The dog chases both of them but they are in no danger. It's quite funny seeing hares standing on their hind legs watching the dog's efforts. When I let him back in he is exhausted and later that night he slept all through Coronation Street, which is his favourite programme. Does this make me a hare courser?

10 July 2021

All the talk, in newspapers and on TV, is of holidays. Where you can go but will have to quarantine when you get back. I must admit that I have not given holidays a thought this year. I know that I am very lucky because I live in such a lovely area and it's no hardship to stay home this year. Others clearly feel the same because I have never seen so many people about as there are now. I was sitting in the car for a while the other day whilst my wife did some shopping and I didn't know one person who walked by. Normally I would know most of them.

I used to love going across to France for a holiday. We used to go across to Brittany; St Malo was always a popular place. The last time we went we sailed from Plymouth to Roscoff. It's quite a long drive from Roscoff to St Malo. I didn't know that you could get a ferry direct from Plymouth to St Malo! It was me that made all the arrangements so I didn't tell the others, who were my wife and a couple of friends of ours. We rented a house in a village just outside St Malo from where we could walk to the old port. Whilst we were unpacking, my friend said he could go to the shop to get some eggs. There was only one shop in the village and it contained the only bar in the village; we were to spend quite a lot of time in there. When he was going to fetch the eggs I reminded him that he couldn't speak a word of French but he said he could mime it. He came back half an hour later – obviously he had drunk several glasses of wine – with a frozen chicken.

Most days we could go to a big nearby supermarket and buy that day's evening meal to cook ourselves. When we walked into St Malo we always passed this really nice restaurant so we decided we would go in there for a bit of a treat. One evening we did just that. It was quite early, we were the only ones in there. When I was at school I lived in fear of the French teacher so I made sure I passed my French exams. If I had had to retake French, well I just would not have gone back. He used to slap children around the head at the slightest excuse and if someone really annoyed him, I had seen him draw blood when he threw a blackboard rubber across the room. I passed French OK but went to do some retakes in the autumn. I was put in with the year below and if they were doing a subject I had passed, I was allowed to sit at the back and not be involved. This included their French lessons with the same teacher. About once a week I would find the teacher standing by my desk. 'You passed French didn't you, come and help me explain this,' Once a week I would end up by the blackboard explaining something I barely understood myself. When he told me to sit down he would wink at me but he would be shouting at all the others. He was one of two teachers at that school who had been prisoners of war of the Japanese; everyone knew they were doing their best. I never used French again for a long time, not until I used to go to France on holiday, and then I was surprised at how much I could still remember. I used to be good at deciding what I wanted to say and if I didn't know those words then I would find a way to say it another way.

Which is how I find myself sitting in this restaurant in St Malo with companions who don't know a word of French. Time to liven things up a bit. The head waiter comes to take our order, and I have to order for everyone. When I have placed the order I tell the waiter that I am a doctor and that I run a psychiatric hospital and the three people with me are my patients. He gives the thinnest of smiles, when he goes back to the kitchen I can see him telling the other waiters. They keep glancing over.

When they serve our meal they keep on laughing nervously. My companions know that I have told the head waiter something about them but they haven't a clue what it is. They laugh nervously as well, which only makes the experience more enjoyable for me. The service was very quick, they can't get us out fast enough. I don't tell them what I had told the head waiter until we are on our way home and it's too late to do anything about it by then.

We spend our last night in France in the shop/bar in the village. It seems that the whole village is there, we knew all of them by now. We have dancing and singing and my friend has his mouth organ with him. He plays Irish songs and I sing them.

17 JULY 2021

Well, I got that wrong didn't I? We had seven Canada geese goslings on our pond and I thought they would all be predated, as they were last year, by birds. Chief culprits are usually Red Kites but there are plenty of buzzards and ravens about. There are two broods on our pond: five that were born here and two that were born elsewhere but were brought here by their parents. That means there are three adults on guard and I suspect this is what has made the difference. I can never get over how the young grow: they are all as big as their parents already and it probably won't be long before they all fly off. I can see the pond when I am sitting down in the evening and there is a fly past of Kites about every quarter of an hour. They do a circuit of the pond just to see if there are any opportunities for a meal. They fly so low and slow you would think they would fall out of the sky.

We have been on the silage recently and the tractor driver reports several hares about. But it isn't all good news because he says that he has seen several leverets carried off by Kites. He has carried some and put them in cover against the hedge but he is sure the Kites watch him and wait for the leverets to reappear.

***

It is Sunday evening and Ann and I decide to go for a drive, to see what wildlife is about. We can drive most places because we have all the cleared silage fields at our disposal. It should be a good evening to see hares. When a field is freshly mown it is the clover that makes the first regrowth and the hares just love some new, fresh, clover leaves. But we get to the field and we haven't seen a hare. Ann says, 'Not much wildlife about.' Then we find out why, because right in the middle of the field is a big red fox. The hares are all probably hiding from the fox and are in the woods. The fox has his head well down, probably mousing, and doesn't hear us coming.

We drive up to him until we are only about thirty yards away then he becomes aware of the truck and dashes for the wood. He is so startled that he crashes through the undergrowth with quite a noise, which disturbs a fallow deer that was lying nearby but which we hadn't seen. We had had reports of a fallow deer that was always on its own but no one seemed to know why. The deer jumps into the wood with one bound, which is what deer do. The wildlife show delivered in the end and I make a mental note to tell the keeper about the fox; it will soon be time for him to have pheasant poults about.

***

This new life takes a bit of thinking about. Yesterday I was driving down a road I have driven hundreds of times. I was noting lots of changes: a new fence around a garden here, a new house there. Then a new mini roundabout at a junction. This all started me thinking, I thought it must be over 12 months since I drove down here. And more than 12 months since I drove anywhere far. We have been out more this last fortnight since restrictions were eased than we've been for over a year, and it feels strange.

It could be the end of the road for my truck. It has its MOT tomorrow. There's warning lights on all over the place. It's been missing badly for over 12 months now. That doesn't bother me, neither does the nasty scrape on the front corner where I ran it down a stone wall on a single track road.

You don't get to know some things about a vehicle until it's too late and you've bought it. First negative I found was when a headlight bulb went. Apparently you have to remove some panels to get at it, so there was a labour charge of £100 just to change a bulb! If you should ever want to get at the battery you have to take the front seat out! It is a wonder the person who designed that can sleep at night. But the thing that bugs me most is the road tax, £580 a year, that is over £10 a week! My son has a 4x4, it is older than mine but has a bigger engine and that's over £200 less. How do they work that out? But the real sin came last weekend. I used the truck all day and it was fine. But we had to go to the village to a barbeque in the evening and it would not start. It turned over OK but it wouldn't fire. It started first touch the next morning as if nothing had happened. I can't do with unreliability like that, unreliability usually carries the death penalty for a vehicle. I have put it in the garage twice, they have put their diagnostic kit on it, and each time they have charged me a £100 to say they cannot find anything wrong with it. I suspect the computer and it could cost thousands to put right.

24 JULY 2021

There was a man who lived in our village who I used to see in the pub. He died far too young. We used to have a private joke that used to bemuse other people. As soon as 24th June had passed, we always used to say to each other 'The nights are getting darker.' And they were, but only imperceptibly, but we always used to say that we could tell the difference. Personally I think the big marker of the passage of time is when the winter barley goes into ear. After that, the year seems to race by and before you know it, she is putting up the Christmas tree.

***

I have got this habit that if someone tells me they are going on holiday I ask them to bring me a stick of rock back.

Not many people have been on holiday lately and as a consequence I've not had many sticks of rock. I don't particularly like rock but if someone is on holiday I like the idea that they are thinking of me. My number two grandson was recently in Newquay so I asked him to bring me some rock back. I didn't think he would but he did and I put it on the shelf by my chair. I like rock best when it goes soft and chewy and this rock was very hard so I left it to age a bit. Last Friday I was watching TV and without thinking about it too much I reached for the rock, intending to take a nonchalant bite out of it. I'm not sure if there's such a thing as a nonchalant bite but that's what I did. It was still very hard but now that I had tasted it I thought I would bite an inch off with my teeth. I bit in to it and there was a cracking noise, louder than rock normally makes when it is broken. I took the rock out of my mouth and one of my front teeth came out with it.

Once, when I was playing rugby, a stray fist or boot removed one of my front teeth. It was fixed eventually by gluing a false tooth to a piece of metal. This piece of metal has two wings to it and these are glued to the teeth that are on either side, dentists call it a bridge. It works well, so well that I often forget it's there.

I've done this sort of thing before. I used to rent some fields where you had to drive down a track to access them. The hedges either side were much overgrown and you could easily reach the hedges out of the truck window. There was a lot of hazel trees growing in the hedge and in the autumn, it was a simple matter to pick some nuts to eat on the way home. These nuts had to be cracked with your teeth. I remember that one nut was particularly difficult to crack and when I eventually cracked it, I cracked three teeth as well. When I spat it out there were bits of tooth and nut everywhere. That particular nut cost me £300 to have crowns fitted. I am now waiting for an appointment to find out how much it costs to bite into Newquay rock.

**

Years ago we went for a family holiday in Carbis Bay, Cornwall. We went before it became so well known. We stayed in a small private hotel which had a tiny bar for residents. There were six of us in our family and when we were in there, there was only room for two more. My brother was not long out of college and one evening we were playing a drinking game. He was in charge and if you made a mistake (in his opinion) you had to drink a 'window' of your pint. The glasses were dimpled pints and a window was about a section, an inch, of that. There was another couple watching us and the man was clearly very amused by it all and eventually asked if he could join in. I should tell you that this other couple fitted exactly the caricature of that married couple that were once seen on those old-fashioned seaside postcards: a large woman and her smaller, hen-pecked partner. We all knew what was happening, even the small man knew what was happening. He made lots of mistakes and had to drink lots of windows but he did it with good humour. His wife, less so, knew he was getting drunk. She had soon had enough and she told him they had better go. He got to his feet and promptly fell headlong onto the floor. She half carried him, half dragged him from the bar by his collar. We never saw them in the bar again but we did see them about, and he always gave us a bit of a smile.

31 JULY 2021

I have never seen so many rabbits on the ground we rent. They do not particularly bother me, there is plenty of grass about. This has happened before. The rabbits become numerous until myxomatosis kicks in and then they die back until there are just a few hardy ones left and then the whole cycle starts again. It usually takes about ten years, from start to finish. There is a lesson in there somewhere but I'm not sure what it is.

***

The locals have been foxing, they always go about now, to have a bit of a clear out before the pheasant poults come. They saw five and shot three. A close neighbour recently had a fox visit her hen coop one night. I would guess that she had around 12 hens. The fox killed the lot and didn't take one. It would feel more forgiveable if it just killed one and took it for food. This wanton sort of killing spree does nothing to endear foxes to country people. It is what foxes do, what they have always done. I still resent the fox that killed 12 cockerels that I reared for Christmas, I was then still at school and that money was going to buy me a new bike. Those who shoot foxes today have very sophisticated rifles, fitted with heat-seeking devices, and they are very efficient, but still the foxes keep coming. Where do they all come from?

Those who count wildlife in the media always intrigue me: they say that a particular species has declined by a percentage. But they don't really know. When someone like Chris Packham is asked, 'Why the decline?' he always puts 'farming practices' in the answer, it's an easy shot but not always true.

***

Our back yard, down to the kitchen door, has got a wall on three side. One of these walls is covered with a creeper, and as long as I can remember it has always been full of sparrows. If I had been asked to guess I would have said there were well over a hundred. Their constant chirping, from dawn to dusk, was a part of our lives. We fed them all our scraps, on a bird table. If I was asked how many were there now, I would say ten. Where have all the others gone?

I once went, as a favour to a friend, to collect three Americans from Heathrow airport. My friend used to run commercial pheasant shoots. He didn't tell me their names or which terminal they were at, he promised to phone me with this information before I got there, but he didn't. I had to park the car and walk into three terminals before I found them. I thought I'd done quite well, it took me two hours, the Americans were very angry because they had sent all this information ahead by email. These wealthy Americans seemed to spend their lives following the seasons around the world, shooting and fishing. They had recently been shooting doves in North Africa and parrots in South America, where apparently you could shoot 3,000 a day if you had a good team of guns! How can you justify such slaughter? Incidentally it was the first time in my life where people would talk about me as if I wasn't there, that's why I never did it again.

***

But I am determined to find out where the sparrows are gone. We have cats up at the farm but the dogs never let them hang about around the house so it's not them. I've haven't spotted American 'sportsmen' lining up a team of guns outside our kitchen. In fact there is only one difference that I can spot. It's a robin, he lives near the back door as well. Our kitchen door is open all day in the summer and he finds his way into the house most days. He is no good at finding the way back out so we usually have to catch him and take him outside. I know that robins are very territorial so perhaps he has chased all the sparrows off. It is the only answer I have at present.

***

There's a sequel to my story about the ramblers who thought that Himalayan Rock Salt were stones and the sheep were eating them because they were so hungry. I get a nice letter from a lady in Wiltshire who came across some similar salt licks. She was so taken with their pink colour that she takes some home to enhance her rockery. Her daughter tells her what they really are, so she takes them back. There is a big difference here. The ramblers were disappointed because they would have liked to report this supposed cruelty to the RSPCA. The lady from Wiltshire is not too precious to pass on a story in which she gets it wrong. This is to be commended.

7 August 2022

My brother and a cousin came to see us. The purpose of their visit is to see some hares and they travel quite a long way to do this. I take them all around the likely spots but we don't see one hare. They are very disappointed but it's a beautiful sunny day and the views are worth a visit, hares or no hares. We are due to start mowing the next day and I tell them that the hares are probably keeping their heads down in the long grass. This turns out to be true. Stephen, who drives our tractor, mows three fields the next day and sees 12 hares in the grass. He keeps an accurate count because he knows I will ask him. The next day after that Ann and I are having our usual ride around and we see a hare. This hare runs about thirty yards in front of us for about 500 yards, it is in no rush and we get a good look at it. Then we see a fox. The fox doesn't hang about and crashes away into the woods. So there is wildlife about even if there are no visitors to see it.

But it gets better. The next day we are driving about the fields that are now cleared of grass. We come across two hares that are chasing each other round and round the field. They are so preoccupied with their chasing that they completely ignore us. Some people say that they are fighting or boxing but I suspect that this chasing is just a prelude to making more hares. The irony is that my two visitors came to see some wildlife but didn't see any. It was there all the time but it chose to keep out of sight.

Later in the week we had a contractor in to round bale some hay during the hot spell. He was quite taken with the deer wandering about amongst the bales. There's plenty of wildlife about, it's just not always about when you need it.

***

We went out for a meal and took a friend and his wife, he's the man who sources our Christmas turkey. The trouble is that he will never tell you how much the turkey is so it has become a tradition that we take them out for a meal to pay for it. They seem quite content with this arrangement, they must be, because the turkey keeps turning up. I still feel a bit mean about the last time. When we took them out last year that meal subsidy of £10 a meal was still on so I had £20 knocked off the price of our turkey. This year I am trying to encourage them to have a starter. The best way to do that is to have one yourself. For reasons that are not clear to me now I decided to have the vegan option, perhaps on the 'don't knock it if you haven't tried it' basis. It was a turnip pate. It tasted a lot like it sounded, it was dreadful. 25p would have been plenty for it, but it cost a lot more than that. I love the ironies in life. Did that vegan starter go in some way to paying for a turkey? Did the cost of the starter pay for a leg, for example?

***

My son-in-law and daughter have this dog around their farm. He's quite unusual for a farm dog, he's nearly all white and he's quite big, about half as big again as your average sheep dog. So I say to my daughter, 'Is that dog any good?' It's the sort of thing farmers say to each other. She says he varies between indifferent and super-efficient, the trouble is that you never know which dog you will get. When he is indifferent there is much barking and huffing and puffing but there are no sheep coming through the gate, so you might just as well have gone on your own in the first place. But when he is super-efficient, you put him around the sheep and he brings the cows and calves as well. He tries to bring the rabbits, the birds and bees. One day he had two ramblers in the sheep pen! If you are minding your own business and going for a walk and you are confronted by a determined dog, going into a sheep pen seems a sensible option.

14 August 2021

There's a big country house close to us, it's idyllic, it is fronted by two long lakes. We go down there four or five times a week, it's so nice. My wife likes to see the swans which she admires, there were rumoured to be 70 there. A month ago there were lots of cygnets about but now there are very few. I stop the truck and ask a lady dog walker I know, 'Where are all the cygnets?' She tells us that there was a rogue male swan, a cob? Anyway, it was killing all the cygnets. If it could catch one on land it just trampled it and if it caught one on the water it drowned it. Presumably not his own children. Nature can be cruel.

***

I've never been afraid to make big decisions. Sometimes you get it wrong but often it's only hindsight that proves it to be wrong and you didn't have hindsight when you made the decision, did you? The bane of dairy farmers' lives used to be when we had milk quotas. Most of us had to buy some or lease some every year and there were lots of factors to take into account because the price of buying and leasing used to fluctuate wildly. If I had to enter this market I used to use the best of my judgement to make a decision and then forget about it.

Lots of farmers used to say to me, 'I leased some quota last week but now it's gone down in price.' I used to make sympathetic noises but in my experience, last week is gone forever, and nothing will bring it back. But the biggest decision is still to be made.

My truck has ended its life here and I was contemplating getting another. It's more of a shed than a truck. I've had it about four years, and it's 12 months since I washed it, I've never cleaned inside but a dirty dog gets in there most days. I hit a stone wall on a single track lane so the front left corner is a mess, I tried to get this fixed on the insurance but they wrote it off. They will now only insure it third party providing I can get it through the MOT, of which more later. Someone clipped the other front corner in a carpark so that's a mess as well. Then there are two additional negatives. It misses badly, has done for over a year. If you are driving along at 40 or 50, it judders which I have got used to, but if it occurs at low revs it will stall and it can take ten minutes to start it again. If this occurs at a junction, which it usually does, other road users find themselves blocked in and they invite you to get out so that they can fight you. My fighting days are long gone.

Sometimes, when there's a big decision to make, you need a bit of a nudge to move you in the right direction. So I put it in for its MOT. It passed without any jobs to do. This completely threw me. I had previously used another local garage until one day I said to the mechanic, 'This car needs an MOT before the end of the month.' He grabbed his MOT pad and started to write an MOT out. I asked him what he was doing. 'It looked OK last time I put petrol in it.' This was good, but it wasn't really, was it? So I took it elsewhere for its MOT and he sent me a bill which I never paid, he didn't press too hard for payment, he couldn't could he? When I go to collect my truck the man gives me the certificate and winks. What do you reckon that was about? I used to buy three-year-old vehicles, now I am looking at ten-year-olds: that's farming for you.

21 August 2021

We went to a wedding recently. As far as I know, this wedding had been arranged three times during lockdown and at different venues, so it's catch-up time for weddings. I had one of those big birthdays a bit back and had decided to have a bit of a 'do'. We didn't go ahead, for obvious reasons. I was talking to the vet and told him that having to cancel was a big saving. He said I should go ahead next year, 'It's only a number with a nought on the end, if it's got a one instead, it doesn't make any difference.'

***

I told you previously that I would tell you this story. We'd had a really good holiday in a rented house just outside St Malo, in Brittany, and now it's our last day and we are driving back from St Malo to Roscoff to catch a ferry back to Plymouth. It's quite a long way to drive and whilst we were away I spotted that you could in fact catch a ferry in St Malo that would take you to Plymouth. My companions, my wife and another couple, who are friends of ours, hadn't spotted this fact and I hadn't told them, so if they read this it will be news to them.

Never mind, it was an enjoyable journey, we stopped to look at some cows, Normandies, and there were fields and fields of aubergines which someone had told us went to New York regularly on a Boeing 747 that was owned by the farmers co-op. At midday we thought we would stop for a break, I can remember that we were driving on a newish duel carriageway and I said we would turn off at the next exit and just keep going until we found a village. We did this but the village turned out to be about five miles away. It was a biggish village all built around what we would call a village green, but this was a big green, perhaps between six and ten acres, it was triangular and was surrounded by houses and shops which had been built so they faced the green.

There was no sign of an inn or bar. I said there was bound to be one here somewhere and we spotted men going into and leaving one of the houses. 'That's either a bar or a brothel,' I said. We went in. It was just like entering someone's living room except that the men in there were either drinking wine or eating, or both. A tiny old lady served us a drink, she spoke good English and told us her daughter had married an Irishman and lived in Dublin. When we ordered our next drink I asked to see the menu. 'We don't serve food,' she said. I said, 'But all these others are eating.' She told me that it didn't work like that. She took me to the door and indicated the shops, 'You go and buy what you want and bring it back here and I will prepare it for you.' So we went and bought some cold meat from the butchers, some salad from the greengrocers and some sticks of bread from the bakers. We gave all this to the little old lady and after just five minutes she had turned it into an attractive meal.

By the time we had finished, all the other customers were gone and she showed us around her house. I was impressed by the double bed which had shutters fixed to it so that when they were shut you slept in a sort of box. She explained that in the past there were large families and children slept in the same room as their parents. The parents would close the shutters to give themselves some privacy. Ever the cynic I couldn't help thinking that if the parents didn't have so much privacy they wouldn't have such a large family, but I didn't say so. This visit was one of the highlights of our holiday, and we who were there often talk about it. But it was all completely by chance. I don't know what the village was called and doubt if I could find it again.

28 August 2021

I'll return to this subject later, because it intrigues me. I hadn't taken much notice of this because I didn't think it affected me, which I know is a selfish attitude. Arable farmers are reporting that there are a lot of wood pigeons about. The arable farmers say that these pigeons are getting together in the sort of big flocks that have not been seen for years and they already fear for oil seed rape crops that they will sow shortly. But it does affect me, as you will see in due course.

***

It's a strange phenomenon, dogs and cars. Your average dog quite likes a ride in a car. But there's a percentage that don't and will be sick every time and they are so reluctant to travel they have to be picked up and placed in a vehicle each time. Then there are the dogs that absolutely love it, for them it is the highlight of their day. My present dog, Gomer, comes into this category. I took him in my truck the day after I had him, when he was still a little puppy and he thought it was wonderful. He used to stand in my lap and help me steer but when we were in the fields I used to put the window down and then he could put his head out of the window. When he got too big to stand in my lap he had to be moved. He was too heavy and people we met couldn't see me and thought he was driving.

He now stands in the back on his hind legs and puts his front legs on the arm rest between the front seats. This is a good place for him to see what's going on. Unfortunately it's also a good place from which to lick my ear.

When I am in the kitchen, the truck is just outside the door, and he spends the day sitting by the truck door, silently begging me to take him for a ride. I take him for a ride most days, we only don't go if there is a lot of rain; I can't bear to see wheel marks on a grass field.

For the first mile of our journey, he makes little whimpering noises of doggy delight. If he were a cat he would probably be purring. It is during these excursions that he gets his daily exercise. Just as soon as we are well away from the road, (he has all the road sense of a hedgehog), I let him out for a run. Our regular journey takes us over a mile and he jogs back behind the truck. He is not losing any weight because he is always eating. But the worst is still to come.

On those days when he doesn't get a ride he spends the evenings just staring at me. After a while this can be very disconcerting. When it starts to get dark and he seems to know that he won't be getting a ride that day, he seems to shrug his shoulders in resignation, climb onto the settee and go to sleep on his back. This is his second favourite occupation. But if he sensed we are going off, he hangs about by the kitchen door and if he can't come, such as when we are visiting friends, or if I have to park up somewhere and it is too hot for dogs to be left in a car, I only have to say 'No,' quietly and he goes to lie under a table. When you get back he is delighted to see you, there is no grudge, he's always been a good natured little dog. We wouldn't be without him. No wonder puppies are so expensive.

***

I've got this good friend who is shortly due a new hip. I phone him up to see how the operation went but he's not due to go in for two weeks. Still it's the thought that counts. Lots of farmers need new hips, their lifestyle pre-determines that. They work very hard, they are out in all weathers, their joints get cold and wet, often both at the same time. This particular friend was an excellent rugby player and if you spend years propping up a scrum, it's about the worst thing you can do for your joints. Just ask my knees!

There was a time in my life when I was involved in the dairy industry and we used to go to 21 agricultural shows a year. We had stands at all these shows. I often used to spend a lot of time standing at the front of these stands, it was a good place to greet people as they walked past. These stands usually had a step up to them which put you slightly above the throng that was walking past. Obviously these people were mostly farming people and from my vantage point, there would always be someone bobbing up and down with the gait of someone who needed a new hip. Every picture tells a story and there in front of you was a very clear indication that a farming way of life was indeed a hard life. I ask my friend if he could bring back his old hip and any other bones that are not needed, for the dog to chew. I can't print his reply but I think it was a no.

4 September 2021

We are not a 'sweet'-driven family. We have our main meal at about six in the evening but we rarely have a pudding. There is an exception to that. At this time of year about once a week, we have raspberries and ice cream. So I say to my wife, 'We haven't had any raspberries lately.' She says, 'It's because the pigeons have had them all.' We are not big on growing vegetables and flowers, my contribution is to keep the lawns tidy, but my wife has some very productive raspberry canes. Some arable farmers reckon there are lots of wood pigeons about. In the past, huge flocks would visit oil seed rape fields, especially in hard weather, and clear them out in just a few days. Oil seed rape is the crop that grows bright yellow later in the year. Come to think of it, pigeons have been the main contributors to the dawn chorus this year. Years ago farmers spent a fortune on devices to scare these pigeons onto someone else's fields but I don't think they were that successful.

I always remember that when the big debate was on years ago, about the benefit or otherwise of GM crops, someone wrote in to a farming magazine and suggested that whilst they were at it, couldn't someone produce a GM oil seed rape that ate pigeons.

So where have all these pigeons come from, it's strange isn't it? We hear of species in decline and it's usual to blame farming practices for this. But if you apply the same logic to pigeons, if there are more about, and there seem to be, because I've been looking, farming should get the praise for this as well. I've got a feeling it doesn't work like that. It's always an easy shot to blame the farmers.

As you might guess, I've got a couple of pigeon stories to tell you. In the late 1960s I had an old man called Bill working here. He told me that when he was a boy he would look for a pigeon's nest and just before the babies fledged they would climb the tree put some string around their legs and tie them in the nests. The parents would continue feeding their young long after they were big enough to fly until they became fat and plump. Then they would make a tasty meal. Most of you will probably think this is a terrible story. But remember that Bill was a boy in the great depression years in the late 1920s and 1930s and there were large families on subsistence wages. Two young wood pigeons would be a welcome addition to a family's diet.

If you think that's a terrible story, here's a worse one. When I was at school I used to help a local farmer on his milk rounds. He had a small farm in the village and about twenty cows which had to be milked. He had two milk rounds, one in the docks which we always did first, and a rural one, which we did after breakfast. We could do the one in the docks relatively quickly because the horses didn't have front gardens to walk up. Then he and I would go back to the farm, have some breakfast, and do some more milk delivery locally.

To set the scene, I don't think I'd be inaccurate if I said the docks were quite a rough tough area in those days. There were feral pigeons around the streets and pavements, and there were boys. These boys were carrying about five yards of fishing line and a hook. In their pockets they would have some bread. What they used to do was moisten the bread in their mouths, put it on the hook and put it on the pavement on the street corner. They would hide around the corner and the pigeons would eat the bread, the hook would go down and the pigeon would be caught. I told you that this as a terrible story. Although we would deliver the milk quite quickly to terraced house, we had an unwritten rule that we never left the truck unattended. If we did we'd probably have had no milk to deliver!

***

We go down to see my daughter on Sunday mornings. My eldest granddaughter has her car up on jacks. 'What's wrong with your car?' 'It needs a new sump.' This is its second sump. I don't think she flattens the sump on speed bumps, it's when the car lands the other side, so that's alright then.

11 September 2021

Our local rugby has come back, post pandemic, with a sort of a bang. There have been four games in eight days. These games are very useful. They give the players a chance to get match fit before the leagues start. We use a mix of players for these fixtures and the games are split into four spells so players can be changed about. And they are useful for the spectators because they give you a chance to get about, something we are not used to. Others must feel the same because there are lots of spectators, for our level, at these trial games. I like to get a look at any new players who may have joined. My eye is on a winger who is particularly quick who I don't know. Turns out he's the vet who did our TB test last week! It's a good thing to have a vet playing, just in case any farmers get injured. Sadly, a couple of players picked up injuries. For them the season was over before it properly began.

***

A casual observer would think I was eating my breakfast, it's beans on toast this morning, and that had my full attention. But I'm watching the TV as well. There's a man on there wearing some red trousers. Red trousers intrigue me, they have almost become a class thing. It seems as if only the 'best' people wear them. I had a pair once and only wore them once – out, that is. I've always had two sets of clothes, one set for everyday, working clothes, and one set to go out in. I have never bought working clothes, I've always down-graded my best clothes to work in. That's not quite true because I've bought new boiler suits. Boiler suits have three qualities: they keep you clean, they keep you warm and people don't know if you have red trousers on! I only wore the red trousers out once to a social function and there was another man there who had some on as well. If I describe him as loud I would be doing him a favour. I remember thinking, 'I hope people don't think of me like that.'

I can't remember why I bought those red trousers, I must have been having some sort of midlife crisis because at about the same time I bought some pink shorts. Those were downgraded to the 'working clothes' department as well but I do remember that I wore them on a holiday in France. I had a big thing at the time about taking too much luggage on holiday so I only took the pink shorts to wear in the daytime and a pair of trousers to travel in and to wear at night. We had a week in Carcassonne with some friends. One day one of the party said she had always wanted to go to the Camargue. I had a look at the map and it was a long way away but I have always liked driving, especially so in France where I enjoy looking at everything. It took us two or three hours to get there but it was well worth it. It turned out to be one of the highlights of our holiday. We came across an inn where our lunch lasted three hours! I only mention this because I wore my pink shorts and people thought I was a flamingo. We saw wild cattle, wild horses as well as the flamingos but the thing that fascinated me were the fields of rice. Before that, I never knew that they grew rice in Europe, nor that I would see it growing.

***

While we are on the subject of clothes I should tell you that when it comes to recycling clothes I lead the way around here. I've never been too proud to wear other people's clothes. I haven't been in a shop for ages but I bet the last one I went in was a charity shop. Charity shops have always fascinated me and over the years I have found some bargains. But now I have found something even better, I get clothes given me by relatives. The shoes I am wearing now were given me by my brother. True, the soles were coming off but we soon fixed that with some super glue. He supplied the pullover as well. The pullover reads like a menu because I usually spill food down it. My trousers used to belong to my youngest grandson. He's only 15 but he's outgrown them. He's the biggest member of our family by some distance. I have a secret wish to get him interested in rugby but so far he shows none. My two eldest grandsons regularly nick my socks but as they never give them back I don't know if that counts as recycling. What I do know is that my relatives all think they are cooler than me and I am quite content in their clothes. All I have on now, that I bought myself are my shirt and my knickers. I'm not sure who the socks belong to. My brother has just bought me some new 'going out' boots at a shop closing down sale. I've not worn them yet but the two eldest grandsons think they are cool; perhaps I will hire them out to them.

18 September 2021

We're at home watching TV. It's time for the adverts; she often uses this opportunity to say something profound, so here we go. 'Out of all the years I've been married to you I've only got one complaint.' We are on dangerous ground now, I'd better tread carefully, so I say, 'What's that?' This is about as honest I've been for some time. 'Out of all the years we've been married, you've never worn a wedding ring.' Phew, I was expecting worse than that. It's a theme she has often raised over the years. I've always said that people could tell I was married just by looking at my demeanour, the grey hair, the drooping shoulders, the lines on my face, the total dejection. But she would never wear that and every so often she will, as now, return to the ring theme.

It's a point I've often thought about but there is something in me that doesn't want to wear a ring. It's very strange because I wear one of those copper bracelets, one of those with magnets in the ends. There was a time in my life when I used to wear a collar and tie most days and my shoulders weren't so good and I couldn't turn the back of my collar down, so I bought the bracelet to see if that would make a difference, and it did. So impressed was I that I also bought off the same firm a device to put over your water supply pipes, which was supposed to prevent the build-up of limescale in your water system. It never worked for us. The bottom of our kettle still looks as if someone tried to make porridge in it.

But here's a strange thing. I had a friend, sadly passed away now, he came from Budleigh Salterton, (I bet that name takes some getting in a stick of rock). He used to go shooting two or three days a week. His pleasure, most of it, came from working his dogs, two spaniels; he enjoyed that part more than the actual shooting. He told me that he would see other dogs on the shoot and that over the years a good dog would not be as spritely as it had been as age began to play its part. In a couple of instances the owners of these dogs bought new collars fitted with the same magnets as my bracelet. He said that the transformation was immediate and dramatic and gave these dogs another two or three years of active and useful life. It's all quite remarkable.

The dogs didn't know what these collars are supposed to do. They can't read the adverts. In my experience spaniels are better readers than Labradors anyway, which is not what you would expect as a spaniel can rarely sit still for long.

Here's what I will do. My daughter does some work with silver as a hobby. I will get her to make a wedding ring, she will sell it to my wife who will give it to me for Christmas and I will wear it. As I said earlier, anything for a quiet life.

25 September 2021

I've decided that I'll get another truck. My truck will become the farm runabout and the present runabout will end up on the scrap dealer's lorry, so you can tell we are not talking about high value vehicles. I've not done anything about finding an alternative because I don't really know what I want. I've always wanted a Range Rover but there's a bit of a stigma attached to them. It's no good if someone calls for some money and you say that you can't pay them until the next milk cheque arrives, and you have a Range Rover parked outside the kitchen door. A friend of mine has just bought a beauty for not much money.

To be honest I am well content with the truck I have now but it needs a new computer and one of those will cost more than I will ever spend on a vehicle. This faulty computer manifests itself in several ways: some days it will go fine; some days it will cut out momentarily so you drive with a serious judder, but I've got used to that; some days it will cut out altogether and can take a quarter of an hour to restart. This usually happens at junctions when you are at low revs and it can get you into bad places.

My grandsons used to borrow it to go rugby training. This had its advantages, from their point of view. They were using my fuel and not their own. They knew that I wouldn't say no if it was rugby related. But their journey takes them on a trunk road and over a level crossing. They have not said as much but I think the engine cut out on the level crossing, they have not asked to borrow it lately. Parking on a level crossing is not a good idea.

The family seem to find it all very amusing, they are all making suggestions. Mostly of the small and sensible sort. Except my daughter who found a 4x4 Porsche for not much money. I said that if I was going to have a Porsche I'd just as well have a Range Rover and she said 'If you are going to change, you should go for it.' I've recently had a road tax bill of £600 a year so I will have to do something by the end of the month.

Life used to be so much simpler. For years all our family and friends used to buy cars from a man I used to call 'my car man'. He was a one-man band who used to buy cars off the trade and sell them on into the trade, that's why they were so cheap. This is how it worked. Every day he would get emails offering him cars.

So if I phoned up and said I wanted a change he would say, 'What do you want?' You would tell him and he would say 'Someone offered me one of those yesterday, I'll phone them and ask about it.' Next day, or possibly next week, he would phone back and say the car was still for sale and did you want to try it for a couple of days. I always said yes because I love driving different cars anyway. In some ways he was ahead of his time, you now see these expensive adverts for car sales on TV. They only do what he was doing all along. He would never tell you how much the car was or how much he would give you for yours, just how much to change. If he did you a favour which he often did, he would ask you to buy him a drink sometime. I don't know what he used to drink but it was £50 a glass. I don't know where he is now because he has moved house and he lives 60 miles away. He didn't tell me where he moved to and he never answers his mobile, so I tell people he's gone to ground.

There was no grandeur to what he did. He didn't have a showroom and his workshop made mine look pristine and mine is a tip. He operated out of a wood and last time I had a wander around there were over 100 cars in the brambles and nettles. I found an Audi car that he'd given my son £1,500 for ten years previously. It was quite a tidy car, the only difference now were the old engine and gearbox and the leather seats were missing.

2 October 2021

There's an owl in the trees in our garden. I'm yet to see it so I don't know what sort it is, but all through the day, about every half hour, it lets out a hoot. It was not very well brought up because it only hoots in the day time, never at night. Everyone knows that owls should only hoot at night. We've got an owl nesting box in a cedar tree and I like to think it's something to do with that but I can see the box quite clearly from where I sit at the kitchen table and I have never seen an owl visit that.

It's a funny old thing, I know the owl is a predator but it doesn't worry me. If it was a buzzard or a red kite I would be worried what it might do. It's a numbers thing, there aren't many owls about so they can't do much harm. Buzzards and kites are everywhere and do. It's all to do with maintaining a sensible balance. I was discussing birds with a farmer the other day and I mentioned kites and he said they are now in decline. Naturally I asked why, and he said that there were now so many they had exceeded their food supply. They are supposed to be scavengers but there is plenty of evidence that refutes that, and now perhaps they will die back to a sensible number.

***

My brother and I were reminiscing about our sister who we have just lost. She had a long illness and we couldn't go to see her because of covid. He was telling me that the night before he was due to start at the grammar school he asked her to cut his hair.

This was big mistake because she had no experience of cutting hair. To keep some sort of symmetry she had to take a bit more off one side to make it match up with the other side so it ended up as a very short haircut. Starting a new school is a difficult time for everyone, all you want is not to be noticed so when my brother says he sidled into his new class, I suspect he positively slunk in there. He identified an empty desk and was just about to sit down when someone called out, 'Hail Caesar!' and so he was known as Caesar until his hair grew back to a more fashionable length. This took about three months.

I've got a similar story to that. A lad I used to play rugby with was always known as 'Acker.' In fact it was some time before I knew his proper name. One day I asked another lad why this lad was known as Acker. He told me that, when they were at school, this boy turned up at school one day wearing a bright shiny waistcoat under his blazer. There was only one other person that wore a bright shiny waistcoat, probably with a Paisley pattern, at the time and that was an entertainer called Acker Bilk. He had a very big hit with a tune called *Stranger on the Shore*. Acker Bilk and his Paramount Jazz Band was what they were called, I think.

Acker Bilk used to play this tune on the clarinet. He always wore a bowler hat and the shiny waistcoat. The teasing was relentless and after three lessons it was time for mid-morning break and the waistcoat was removed and stuffed into his locker. But the name stuck. Only last year someone who doesn't live around here anymore was asking about his old rugby teammates. He asked me 'Do you ever see Acker?' So the name has stuck for thirty years and he only had the waistcoat on for just over two hours!

9 October 2021

Naturally I went to my sister's funeral. She had had a terrible last two years. In and out of hospital, in great pain, living on her own, in a wheelchair, she showed great bravery and fortitude. Her children lived close by but couldn't go to see her because of covid. We intended to go and stay with her two or three times a year, to give her some company but couldn't for the same reason. It all serves to put some perspective on life. Her late husband's brothers were all at the funeral although she'd been widowed these seven years, and they had to come a long way. When we left we all said, 'See you again' although now the connection is gone I doubt we ever will. But life goes on and I turn my attention to my own brother.

We all know that what he wears today I wear tomorrow. He's got a grey suit on that I have always fancied but I've got plenty of suits, five including the one I have on. This is the only one I can get into and that's a struggle. But that doesn't really matter, five suits look good in your wardrobe. When I was in my 20s I bought a brown pin striped suit with flared trousers. I kept it for years. I thought that one day I would wear it for fun. One day I was having a bit of a clear out so I tried it on, the trousers were six inches away from meeting properly. I can't remember what I did with it, I often wonder if someone still has it. I wish I'd kept it for my grandsons, it would fit them. Back to my brother, his black shoes are better than mine but they look quite new so they will probably see him out. I wonder if he wants his car....

***

Let's put some detail on this. The nearest house to the pub adjoins it, on the same side of the road. The second-nearest house is right opposite on the other side of the road, part of a development of about ten bungalows that were built some years ago in a field. What is the distance of this bungalow, from the pub? Well there's the width of the road and a lawn, altogether about 10-15 yards, you get the general idea, this bungalow is close to the pub, it always has been. A couple of months ago this bungalow changed hands and the new owner has already been complaining about the pub noise. You can't believe it can you! It's true that the pub has been busy of late, I've never seen so many tents and caravans on the campsite at the rear but I think that could be a lot to do with people taking their holidays in this country. I suspect that it will be a lot quieter when the winter comes. One of the troubles is that this new resident has put all the complaints on social media, so everyone knows.

There have been some very robust comments and replies. Obviously I don't know how long the new bungalow owner will stay there but it is not a good way to get to know your new neighbours. Some locals have given it both barrels in their replies. It's a bit like when you read of someone complaining about church bells when they have just bought a house next to a church, or people around here complaining about farming activity. There was a letter in the local press last week complaining about tractors on the roads. When they moved here, what did they think went on in all those fields? A big story these days is of food shortages. If they restrict tractors on roads, then you would see some empty shelves! People just don't think things through. They see what they see as a problem and never ask themselves any questions, the why and the wherefores.

16 October 2021

I thought that the sheep industry would be the first casualty when we left the EU because so much of their output finds its way into Europe. I got that completely wrong: sheep prices this year have been at record levels. I know farmers that sell yearling breeding ewes at this time of year, they always have done, and if you had told them two or three years ago that they would get over £200 for them, they would never have believed you.

Autumn is the start of the sheep year, it's when you buy ewes and tups. I haven't had sheep for years but I used to love going to sheep sales, and I still miss it. The last ewe sale I went to was with a friend of mine; he wanted to buy some Nelson ewes. Nelson is a village in the south Wales valleys just south of Merthyr. Around there they have their own sort of Welsh ewe. They are slightly bigger than the normal Welsh ewe, they are very good milky mothers and have a reputation for escaping out of anywhere. They will climb over fences, they will climb over gates. If they can't climb over a gate, they will lie on their backs and wiggle under it. They mostly have a tan face, which distinguishes them. At the sale, several ewes had jumped out of their pens and were making their way back up the mountain. No one seemed too bothered by this. One lady who was selling ewes told me that if you had one in the freezer, not to leave the lid open too long or it would jump out!

***

I well remember the last time I bought some tups. I needed two but I bought three. The very last thing you need in a tup is if it injures itself fighting. It's usually ok if they clash heads, they seem to do that all day and there is often a fearsome crack but rarely is harm done. What you don't want is for them to miss their heads and hurt their shoulders or if one turns away and gets a blow to its back leg. When these tups are serving ewes you want them mobile, you don't want them on three legs. If you went to a sale there was a good chance that you would buy tups off different vendors and they would then fight. They never seemed to fight in the trailer where you could keep them separate and if you couldn't, the motion of the trailer and keeping their balance seemed to preoccupy them. They fought when they were put into the field.

But I used to give this fighting some thought. In my workshop I had five gallons of clean sheep dip and a watering can. The theory was that strange tups would fight anyway, because they didn't like the look of the other tups. But if they all smelt the same, they wouldn't fight as much. So I filled the watering can up with sheep dip before I went and the idea was that I would put some dip on the tups before I let them out into the field and they wouldn't fight so much because they all smelt the same.

I bought two yearling tups and a four-year-old. An old aunt had told me years ago 'always have plenty of tups, boy!' I need to put some perspective on this and although I can't remember what I paid, it was £300-ish for the yearlings and £60 for the four-year-old, it was that sort of proportion. When I got them home I let them into a loosebox and went straight away to fetch the watering can, which was only next door. How long was I away: ten seconds, maybe 30? Certainly not a minute. When I got back, the two yearlings were dead. The four-year-old had the whole watering can of dip over him but I doubt it taught him a lesson. I had to go and buy another tup the next week. I only bought one this time and I only paid £60 for it. Sheep farming was ever thus.

23 October 2021

A friend of mine gets in touch. She and her husband are sort of retired from farming now but still lamb some ewes. They live where they have always lived, in a small village that used to be a collection of small farms and houses that were used by people who worked in a rural community. The farms are nearly all gone now, theirs is the only one left, and the houses are owned by second home owners, or people who have retired, and the bigger houses do B&B. I'm not saying that there's anything wrong with any of that but it's a small village and it's a bit out of proportion, the balance has gone. They have lived there longer than all the others put together. I'm not sure if it is a hamlet or at what point a hamlet becomes a village or when a village becomes a small town.

But the problem for this long-time resident is that all the people that now live in her locality are vegan or vegetarian and she and her husband don't feel part of the community anymore. They feel ostracised and if they should be out walking they are more likely to get a snide remark than a 'good morning', which is a shame.

Anyway, a car arrives on their yard driven by a lady that they know has bought a cottage a couple of fields away. The lady gets out of the car, there's no introductions. 'I live in that house there, it overlooks your yard, I watch you all the time through my binoculars. I watched you all through lambing in the spring and you need to know that I shall be watching you every day.' My friend was going to invite her new neighbour in for coffee but there was no time for that. 'I have seen some of your sheep limping, I shall report all that in future.' Sheep love to limp, especially if someone is watching. I've seen people limping in hospital car parks, it doesn't mean that they haven't been treated in A&E, limping doesn't get cured instantly.

But that's only the start. 'Do you castrate your lambs with rubber rings?' 'Yes.' 'You will need to stop that!' No discussion, a clear instruction, we have here some audacity, some ego! 'Do you use the same rubber rings to shorten the lambs tails?' 'Yes' 'You must stop that as well.' Finally my friend gets a word in, 'but when the lambs are bigger and if their tails become soiled or wet, blow flies lay their eggs on them, the eggs quickly turn to maggots and the maggots will eat the sheep alive, which is much worse than a rubber ring.' She was wasting her time, the lady isn't listening. 'When you are moving the ewes and lambs about you carry the lambs by their front legs, that will have to stop.' If you are moving ewes and lambs the only way to do it is to dangle the lambs by your side so the ewe can see and smell her lamb. Lambs have been moved like this for centuries, it doesn't hurt them, and is the best way to do it. Trying to drive newly-born lambs is a bit like trying to herd cats, it's best avoided.

Being told how to do it, by someone who has never ever done it, goes against the grain. If you cradle a lamb in your arms, the ewe can't see it or smell it and is likely to run back whence it came, which is the last thing you want.

My friend tells me that they get the blame for everything. These new people don't recognise their tractor, so if there's a tractor doing something they don't like, it's down to them. They were blamed for cutting the roadside verges when it was clearly the council. A big combine was making its slow way through the village, they had the blame for that although they don't grow any corn! This village will get cut off if there is a big snow and these newcomers haven't got a clue how to drive in deep snow, bet the tractors will be a good thing then! Some of the people who move into the countryside think it was designed by Enid Blyton and packaged by Mothercare and that it should fit around their vision and not around the real world, the life-and-death world, of the people already there.

Besides, isn't watching someone all day through binoculars close to stalking?

30 October 2021

One of the biggest changes to farming over the last generation or so is that of potato growing. There was a time when a lot of farmers grew just one field of potatoes every year. The prices of the potatoes they grew would fluctuate wildly from season to season. This would largely be due to the weather. If it was a dry year, yields would be down and prices would be up. All that has changed now and potato-growing is largely in the hands of big growers who run huge operations. A feature of this is that potatoes must not be grown on the same land for five consecutive years so these growers seek out 'clean' land to rent off other farmers. Some of these growers may grow 1,000 acres of spuds and some of the fields they rent may be as far as 30, 40 or even 50 miles away from their stores. That's why you often see tractors and trailers loaded with potatoes criss-crossing the countryside in the autumn every year. As usual I have stories about this.

One farmer I know who was growing well over 1,000 acres, up to 50 miles away from home, thought he would run things 24 hours a day because conditions were so good.

To understand this all better, you need to know that all the potato tractor drivers involved would be cocooned in their cabs and would only get out for a call of nature or if something broke. For example the man on the harvester would have a succession of tractors and trailers pull up alongside him and he would fill the trailers and never speak to the drivers. So they are working 24 hours a day and the drivers are working 12-hour shifts and the work is from 8am to 8pm at night. Thus at 8am the boss arrives with a diesel bowser to supervise the changeover and whilst the diesel is going in, the driver of the harvester says to his boss, 'Is that blue tractor on trial?' The boss says there is no blue tractor involved. The driver of the harvester says that a blue tractor came three times in the night and took three loads of potatoes away! It was clearly a driver who had got lost. They never did find out who had had three loads of potatoes.

The big prize in this search every year for clean ground is the chance to irrigate, so if there is a river or a big pond handy, they will pay more. One of these big potato growers rents some fields, there isn't any water about but there's a river flowing through the field the other side of the road. He does quite big mileage in the spring and if he sees a dead badger on the road he picks it up and puts it in the truck. He puts these dead badgers on this road. When there are about six there, he phones the highways authority. They come out and he says that the local badgers were crossing this road regularly as part of their normal activities and lots of them were getting run over and killed. As we all know, the word badger is one of the most emotive words in our language; at its mention all common sense disappears. In no time at all the council had closed the road, dug it up, and put a big culvert in for badgers to travel. Of course there were no badgers, there was no nearby sett, and the culvert was a waste of taxpayers money. But it was very handy to run some irrigation water pipes through and to get some water out of the river for the potatoes! As far as I know that is all it was ever used for.

The wily potato grower had outwitted the highways authority, the authority was fine with that because they had the very best of intentions and the consumers would be ok because irrigated ground grows more potatoes. And who knows, perhaps the culvert will be used by a passing badger in the future.

6 November 2021

I don't know why but I've been thinking a lot about my school days lately. Particularly of when I entered the fifth form. I think that they call it year eleven now. It was when you entered the fifth form that big decisions were made.

To start with you could end the year by leaving school if you so wished. This was to be the biggest decision you had ever made, never mind that your parents might have a view. The fifth form was when privileges started to appear in your life. At my school you could wear a tidy jacket instead of a blazer and you were allowed to leave the premises at lunchtime and go for a walk. Although bizarrely, you were still expected to wear a cap. If the head was doing a uniform inspection at the gates when you went home, it meant a mad dash back to the cloakroom to see if you could find a cap. Or if you were in the fifth form, you could snatch a cap off a first former and give it him back later and he would have to scour the cloakroom for another. I never did this, never been very good at taking advantage of weaker people. If I couldn't find a cap I would keep out of sight until the head got bored. It was a highlight, for me anyway, that if the lunch hour was wet, you could go to dancing lessons in the hall. Most of my friends didn't go dancing and went for a walk as usual and got wet as a consequence.

The highlight for me was that you could hold the hand and put your arm around the sixth form prefect that you were seriously in love with, but she wouldn't even speak to you normally when you passed her in the corridor on a normal school day. But mostly we used to go for a walk and talk endlessly about our futures and what lay in store for us. It was the year we would sit our O levels (GCSE's) and we all thought that we would get five or six. I was only to pass three as it turned out, but I needed six to get to the agricultural college I had chosen. I had the chance to do some tractor work in the evenings when the exams started so I didn't tell my parents they were on. It was the wake-up call I needed and I went back to school and passed three more fairly well.

When we went for those walks we all thought that we would pass five or six and so we had a fall-back position. Every night in the evening paper there was an advert. It said 'Customs Officers wanted, five O levels' and it stated the salary which was ok. So we all said that we could become customs officers if we needed to, there was plenty of work in the South Wales ports of Newport, Cardiff and Barry.

As it turned out I don't think any of us became customs officers. There were two boys in our class, I'm not saying they were dishonest, but they were a bit shifty. They were the only boys in our class that used to smoke behind the bike sheds. Next time I saw them they were directing traffic; they had joined the police. Several of my friends became teachers as the main exports from South Wales in those days were coal, steel and teachers. My brother and sister became teachers but they were a lot brighter than me.

I had to manage as best I could with all the good looks, the charm, the personality, and the modesty I was blessed with. My siblings were both good artists as well. My brother puts his paintings for sale down by his garden gate and then spends all his time worrying in case someone nicks one.

I can't remember a time when I didn't want to be a dairy farmer. I thought that there would always be a living for those who produced nature's most natural and wholesome food. When we went organic I thought that was even more true. I got that wrong, didn't I? we are getting less now for our milk than we were getting three or four years ago. How long do you think we can do that?

13 November 2021

News comes in of a dairy farmer's wife who drives her children to school one day. Unknown to her the area is crawling with radar vans to stop speeding drivers. She triggers two vans on her way to school and two on the way back, so by the time she gets home she has 12 points and loses her licence. I don't know if this story is true but why spoil a good story with the truth? People always like a story of someone else's misfortune.

I used to do a lot of driving to farmer's meetings when I represented the dairy industry. These used to take me all over the country and involved a lot of driving late at night. I had two criteria that were important to me. One was that I would never leave for home as long as there were members in the room. This often meant that I would start for home at 10.30 or 11pm. And I would always drive home if I could get home within three hours. I could have stayed in a B&B somewhere but that would eat into the next day and I liked to keep the expenses down. Celine Dion and I have travelled many a mile together late at night. There were two dangers to overcome: one was not to fall asleep; and the other was long villages.

One night I attempted a drive home of five hours. This was too far and to keep awake I bought two or three cans of red bull. The trouble with that was that when I got home I couldn't get to sleep! By long villages I mean those you aren't familiar with that go on for a couple of miles with a 30mph restriction and speed cameras about. That's how I ended up with six points on my licence, and another case pending.

The thought of nine points on your licence focuses your mind. Never mind that I had only done about 38mph in each case, that it was early in the morning and there was nothing about. That's why I was very happy to forgo the final three points and to go on one of those speed awareness courses. There were about twenty of us involved, the man in charge sat us in a circle and we had to answer some questions in turn. I can't remember all the questions, but I know they included what sort of car you drove, how many miles, and what did you think was the biggest danger on the road? He started with the person next to me and went the other way around so I was to be last. They all said that they drove expensive cars, mostly German imports, of which more later. About the third to speak said that the biggest danger on the road was farmers. The other must have been very short on imagination because they all picked up on the anti-farmer theme.

And so we get, finally, to me. I said that the course was anti-farmer and therefore not PC, in fact, (and I stood up), it was ethnic cleansing of the very worst sort and I was thinking of going, and reporting it. The man in charge was beside himself. He was obviously fearful of running a meeting that was accused of not being politically correct. There were people there from all walks of life but no one spoke to me after my outburst, they, including the man in charge, hadn't the wit to work out that I was just winding them up.

When it finished I was first out, they were all chatting but no one was chatting to me. I expected to see lots of expensive cars in the car park but I didn't. The best car was the big old Honda that I had for three years and had bought at a car auction for £2,700! So when they were asked at the start of the meeting what they drove, they were all fantasists, which is a kind way of describing someone who tells lies.

20 November 2021

Doctors have been in the news seemingly every day lately, mostly GP's and mostly for the wrong reasons. I've never troubled my doctor very much, working on the principal that a doctor's waiting room was a good place to catch something. But I go every year for my flu jab, which is mostly administered by a nurse, and I try to go for what I call my annual MOT but it is mostly every two years. I know the one doctor quite well, I used to play rugby against him and he lived down 'our' lane in a cottage for several years. If we meet on the street we always stop for a chat, though these days I am more likely to meet him on a footpath over our land. He is a second generation doctor, his late father was our doctor as well.

I once had to speak at a local dinner and reply on behalf of the guests; the doctor was one of the guests. No matter what your ailment, this doctor was well known for giving tetanus injections. I remember going to see him one morning with a broken collar bone that I had acquired late the previous night on licenced premises. I was in agony.

These days if a member of the medical profession asks you to describe pain, they ask you to put it on a scale of one to ten. You can't say ten because you will never know if you've been there but this collar bone was definitely an eight. It had hurt me all night and all I wanted was some pain relief, but the doctor was looking through my records to check on my tetanus status.

At the dinner I said that the local medical practice had got a mention in the *Guinness Book of Records* because the people around here had the highest tetanus status in the world. It got a very good laugh because everyone knew what I was alluding to. I didn't see that particular doctor for a long time. It's not for the faint-hearted to have a doctor bearing down on you with a needle in his hand who says 'I went to a dinner last year and you took the mickey out of me.' The less charitable of you are probably thinking that he was paid for every injection. I've got a medical condition that I didn't used to have when I was younger. Getting older is not for the faint-hearted. The last time I saw the doctor, I asked him a perfectly sensible question and he told me to google it. What sort of answer is that?

***

It's been a sort of year for lawn mowing. At times the grass has grown prolifically, at others the lawns have been burnt and brown. I had to buy a new mower last year and I don't enjoy this one as much as the old one. The old one had a cutting deck at the front and you could cut around trees, in the corners etc but those sorts are very expensive so I opted for the cheapest. Riding on a mower always looks a comfortable occupation but by far the best advantage is that you can drive right over dog poo and you don't get any on you. This new mower would always start first time, an admirable quality in a mower, but when I got it out last week it started ok but it wouldn't cut.

I called for help and we found that rats had been chewing the wires. Rats can be a problem on a farm especially in the autumn when they are looking for somewhere warm and dry to spend the winter. I wouldn't want you to tell anyone else this, but last year some rats got into the house. Of course this was my fault. I quite like creepers up the outside wall, and I have been told thousands of times that rats can use these creepers as ladders and climb them and enter the house via the eaves. On one memorable occasion, a rat crossed the kitchen when we were having breakfast. Rats don't bother me but they can cause panic in others. My wife threatened me with divorce and physical injury if I didn't do something about it. I've got some good stories about rats, I'll tell them next time.

27 November 2021

Before I was married I was a herdsman on a farm but I used to help out with all the other farm jobs as well. On this farm they had two sheds that contained what were called 'breeder chickens'. They went to supply hatching eggs to a nearby hatchery. The sheds were largely deep litter, it's where the cockerels and hens would go for hanky panky. Down one side would be all the nest boxes. One shed had brown egg producers. These would go broody and peck your hands to pieces when you collected the eggs. The other shed housed white birds that were a bit flightier, that laid white eggs. The cockerels in this shed would queue up to attack you whilst you collected the eggs. Down the length of the other side of the shed was a raised slatted area, about four feet high, and on here were the drinkers and feeders and the birds roosted on here as well.

There were rats below these slats, it was a good place for a rat to live. There was ample food and water and the litter would be warm and dry except where the drinkers had been leaking! All of these sheds had to be cleaned by hand when the birds went but I don't remember ever minding, that was just how we did things in those days.

So the birds are gone and we know there are lots of rats below the slats. At the time my mother had a dog, a mongrel, she was smaller than a sheepdog, and she was white all over. We called her Snowy (no shortage of imagination in our family). There's two things I remember about Snowy. In the autumn she used to spend her time around the hedgerows, eating blackberries, until her head was purple; and she was good on a rat.

One day the boss said to me, 'After you come back from breakfast we'll make a start on those chicken sheds.' And I said 'I'll bring my mother's dog, she might catch a rat.' In the event she caught lots of rats. She was in a fair old mess; when she chased some of them they ran through the pools that had accumulated under the drinkers, and these pools were now nothing more than liquid chicken poo, and boy did she smell. At lunchtime we laid all the rats out that she had caught and she had caught 97. I took her home and she was so exhausted, she sort of crawled into her basket and didn't get out for two days. I wanted to take her in again in the afternoon but my mother wouldn't let me. In fact, she never let me take her anywhere again.

***

There was a story I heard of a farm that was plagued by rats so they decided to do something about it. They got a gang in one night, there were lots of terriers and the gang had chainsaws with the cutter removed. The idea was that they could then place the engines close to a rat hole, blow the exhaust fumes down a hole, the rats would come out to escape the fumes and the terriers would catch the rats. They say they caught 400 but this story gains 50 rats every time it is told.

***

Got to tell you this. I've not done anything about swapping my 4x4. In fact I've taxed it for another six months. I asked a local man to find me another but he didn't, so I taxed it. You've not seen stubborn or bloody minded until you've met me! Just to recap, my 4x4 has been playing up for many months, it cuts out momentarily as you are driving along. It has been juddering from A to B but I have got used to it. A bigger problem has been when it cuts out at low revs because it is difficult to start again. So we are driving on a B road and joining a busy trunk road at a roundabout and it stalls and takes 15 minutes to get it going again. This means the trunk road is blocked in one direction for 15 minutes, the traffic was queuing as far as we could see, and nothing could get out of the B road. What really surprised me was that we didn't get any angry gestures or horn blowing. The 4x4 has been going without a judder for two days now. If it goes ok I'll keep it, it suits me just fine. It isn't very green but then neither is junking it.

4 December 2021

This happened to me yesterday, it could easily happen to you. Every Sunday morning we go to see our daughter. So, because it looks a bit frosty outside I put my fleece on. Into the pocket of the fleece I put the car keys. We get in and shut the doors, so far so good. But it isn't. I've shut my fleece in the door, not normally a big deal. The pocket with the keys is half-jammed in the door, and because the door-shutting has activated the key fob, the doors are all locked. We can't open the doors because they are locked and we can't open the windows because you need to switch the ignition on to do that and we can't switch the ignition on because, as you know, the keys are jammed in the door. This dilemma lasts for twenty minutes until eventually I phone my son.

This is not as easy as it sounds. Members of my family rarely answer the phone to me because I've usually got a job for them. He comes to the car. Then we have to shout to my son through the closed windows, just where he will find the spare keys. They are in 'my' drawer in the kitchen, but so are every set of spare keys that I've had for years, so we don't tell him that. There's all sorts of things in my drawer, there's lots of photographs which have all been waiting for years to be put in a better place. I was once on a safari in Zimbabwe and I found a piece of pottery in an abandoned village; that's there as well. But the most precious of all are some bits of twigs. My eldest granddaughter was here one day, she had just learned to walk and she went around our garden for the first time on her own. She brought me back those twigs and I still have them; they have been there about twenty years. But the spare keys are the main thing today and he has managed to find them. Of course this was all my fault and I've been forbidden to wear that fleece again.

***

I remember telling you the dog Gomer was staring at me in the evenings. Well this is worse since the evenings have got darker. He often sits about three yards in front of me for hours. He never blinks or turns away. He doesn't turn to watch the soaps anymore. It's all very disconcerting. He could be waiting for a tit bit, which I sometimes have. A grape or a piece of apple. A Fisherman's Friend or a Rennie, all of which he eats with relish. Do you think that he's trying to hypnotise me?

11 December 2021

My eldest grandson is mumbling to himself in the kitchen. He is mumbling expletives so I won't repeat them. We recently had a dairy farm assurance visit and he is accumulating photographic evidence that we have put right any wrongs they have found. There are over 80 pages in our assurance book, I wonder how many pages there are if you farm livestock elsewhere in the world or if they even have a book! I've given what I am about to write a lot of thought but will go ahead anyway because if I am to compete with New Zealand farmers, there are things you should know. I know a lot of farmers who have spent time in New

Zealand. You can easily spot them because, like a lot of postmen, they wear shorts in the winter.

A sole farmer in New Zealand looks after vast quantities of sheep, for example, one man can be in charge of say 7,000 sheep. In fact there are so many that at busy times he will only have time to visit each flock once a week. Can you imagine that at lambing time? But there is a natural selection process at work here. If the sheep can't survive a management system that involves the very minimum of attention then they just die and their genes die as well, so those who survive will only produce sheep suited to the system.

And that, in a way, encapsulates how livestock is managed in some other countries around the world. Countries like Australia, New Zealand and the Americas. It's a numbers game and the profits are based on how the whole herd or flock can cope. I can see why some parts of society dislike farmers as a result. I am heartily relieved that UK farmers don't have to farm by numbers and it will be a very sad day if we are ever pushed to farm like this. So next time your hand is raised to lift a product off the supermarket shelf, just ask yourself how it was produced and where it came from. I readily admit that I've never been to New Zealand and I've not seen any of these bad practices. But I've been told by people I trust who showed me photographs, and they were as appalled as I am.

18 December 2021

My wife is by the window in the kitchen so I ask her how old my ailing truck is. She looks out and works out, '15 years'. This is a bit of a blow, I thought it was only 14. An expert on number plates is my wife, she always knows what the new numbers are and when they change. It's much too complicated for me. We did have a new car once when the plate changed; it was a T reg in the late

70s and inflation was so high then, you could buy a car and run it for 12 months and it would be worth more money. Not that I can remember that doing anyone any good.

***

One year we had a three day break in Torquay and after breakfast we went down the hill to the harbour for two reasons. Firstly for me to see the boats, I like looking at boats. Secondly to make sure that the sea was still there; when you are a farmer you don't take anything for granted. My wife says to me, 'It's the new number plates today,' (it must have been the 1st of August). The one of us that sees a new number plate first has to give the other £1.' I said, 'I need to cross the road here.' 'Why?' 'I want to look at the cars in that Volvo garage.' It was as easy as that. There in the forecourt were three new cars with new registrations, awaiting collection. She gave me £3 but I think she still resents it. Come to think of it, I don't think I have made any easier money since.

***

I've asked people about my car billowing smoke, people with more mechanical knowledge than me. It's not difficult to find people with more mechanical knowledge than me. Thus far I've had three theories offered. The first said it was the air filter, another the fuel filter, the third the turbo. With vehicles that need attention, the correct diagnosis is the key. Me, I've got an idea of my own, an idea which gives me no comfort at all. I used to park the lawn mower next to the car and rats trashed the wiring on the lawn mower. Could be that they've been at the car as well. In fact it would be a surprise if they hadn't. We have never had trouble with rats over the years because cats are the solution to that. We've always had plenty of cats, true, they've been feral cats, which means amongst other things, you could never get near them. But we always used to feed them. Milk twice a day and biscuits once. It takes a fine healthy cat to tackle a big rat.

We used to get visits from itinerant tom cats who used to keep the kittens coming. A lot of the kittens used to die with cat flu but you could never catch them to do something to help. Sometimes the cats would produce the most beautiful 'blue' kittens, I don't know where that strain came from. I think we only have two cats at present, and it's clearly not enough.

December 2021

More about vehicles. I had this car once, I used to do a lot of miles in it so I looked after it, had it serviced and the like. It used to live outside our kitchen. I had one of those personalised number plates on it that included the letters MOO! Get it, a dairy farmer and moo! My daughter had the car after me and she still has the number plate. I never got caught speeding in that car, because in those days you could buy an aerosol that you could spray on your plates and not be recorded on cameras. These sprays became illegal. For me that was quite a big breaking of the law, never been one who is comfortable doing something wrong.

Anyway, when that car went for a service, on several occasions they found that mice had made nests in the air filter. I used to give a lot of thought to those mice as I drove along. When I got to my destination did they get out for a look around, or did they sit tight until I went home? If they got out they could be left behind and would find themselves in Pembrokeshire or somewhere else in west Wales or even in Carlisle or Glasgow. But I didn't lose any sleep over it, they had no business setting up home in my air filter. Besides, when the car mechanics crawl all over your car with their laptops trying to diagnose any faults it might have, I bet there isn't a display on their laptops that says 'have a look in the air filter, there's some mice living in there.'

Just before I had this car I had a van, and the van had a mirror affixed to the door. There was a spider living behind the glass of the mirror and as far as I know he was there for three years. We did miles and miles together. It can't be an easy life, living behind the mirror of a Transit van so in the winter I used to catch him things and he used to come out to fetch them. I called him George, I don't know how he identified himself or whether it was correct for me to put a gender on him (you can't be too careful these days). Perhaps he had a preferred pronoun. But there's a fair chance that, like, most of us he didn't know what a preferred pronoun is or was. When I sold the van I never gave a thought to George and he probably ended up in a crusher. I still feel a bit guilty that I sold him (or her) with the van. It must have been the sight of all that cash that distracted me. It wasn't all cash, there was a balance that was paid by cheque. The cheque bounced, it was an account that had been closed for 12 months, but I didn't follow it up.

***

Our Christmas tree went up in November this year, very little gets past me. My granddaughter put it up, I tried to get her to put it down the fields but she passed on that. When I think of Christmas I often think of a raffle I helped to organise, with a friend, for the rugby club. It was one of those big raffles that you rarely see these days with about twenty prizes. It was a lot of work. First you had to get the prizes, then you had to get the tickets printed, then you had to distribute the tickets and then you had to get the money and the counterfoils in, and on it went. We'd had enough long before the end. Just the two of us did the actual raffle and eventually we got down to the last two prizes. A pair of tights went to a person five miles away and a turkey went to a person in Blackpool. In the circumstances we thought it would be eminently sensible to swap these prizes over, so we took the turkey five miles and put the tights in the post and sent them to Blackpool. I know it was wrong. We thought no one knew but it was such a good story it got out and someone reported us. We had a letter from the licensing authority, 'You will never be allowed to do a raffle again.' Suits us just fine. We didn't intend to do another anyway.

1 January 2022

I used to have a good friend, who has been passed away these 12 months now, who kept meticulous records of our rainfall. I've always been interested in the weather, good or bad, weather can make or break your farming year so I used to ask him regularly what had been going on.

I once had my own rain gauge and affixed it to a fence on the yard but it didn't last long. It was smashed down by the loader on a passing tractor; the driver said he didn't know it was there. It had lasted about an hour. I've always been pragmatic, it wasn't meant to be, so I shrugged my shoulders and continued to ask my friend, until he died and I knew I would have to do something. I can't remember if it was my birthday or Father's day, but my daughter asked me what I wanted and I said 'a rain gauge' thinking it would be inexpensive.

A white van duly turned up with quite a sophisticated rain gauge. I didn't know that such a thing existed but it's in two parts. You put one outside, ours is about ten yards away on a wall, in our garden. And it measures the rain as it falls so you never have to empty it. The other part is a digital display that sits on our kitchen table. It's supposed to tell you how much rain has fallen but it also tells you the outside temperature and the inside temperature. We've never got the rainfall function to work, an important part of a rain gauge's job. It is probably due to my bad habit of throwing away instructions with the packaging, a habit that has caused me considerable difficulty in the past.

But not to worry, I find the temperature information fascinating. The warmest room in our house is the kitchen because we leave the Rayburn on day and night. When I get up it's always on 13 degrees. I give the central heating a blast for an hour every morning so the kitchen creeps up to 15 degrees, if it's a nice day outside it sometimes hits 16 degrees. What goes on outside is of more interest. To the south of us about half a mile away, is a big hill. The sun hides behind this in the early mornings but on sunny days, when it rises above the hill, the temperature outside puts on about three degrees in about five minutes. This hill is covered with larch trees, always has been ever since we've been here, but if they were to fell these trees, the hill would be lower and we would get the sun five minutes earlier in the morning. Could be that if there were no trees, the grass would grow a week earlier in the spring? It's a bit strange isn't it, that when most people are talking about planting trees, I am pondering the side-effects of cutting some down? I'm sure that if they cut them down, they would plant some more, isn't that what renewable means?

***

We've had a big oak tree come down in the middle of a field, in the storms. It's a shame but there you go. It was a funny shape and I always thought it was vulnerable to a storm. About ten years ago I had a tree surgeon tidy it up a bit, make it more symmetrical, particularly one big branch which stuck out at an angle. I should have asked him to cut it harder but it's down now and too late. We probably won't cut it up until the spring, when the ground dries up. I know of one big estate that always plants a new tree whenever one comes down. That's a good idea, perhaps we will do the same. It means that the estate will look the same in 100 years as it does now, with lots of trees about. Lots of trees around here are reaching the end of their life, there can't have been much tree planting going on 50 or 60 years ago. There's an avenue of Turkey oaks on a road around here and it always makes me sad to see one felled but they are always rotten in the trunk and therefore unsafe, especially next to the road.

***

Just had a message from a reader that warns me of the dangers of feeding grapes to dogs. Over the years I have been amazed at some of the things our dogs will eat. Their mentality seem to be: 'I'll eat this just so that another dog doesn't,' there is a competitive element to it all. I'll always remember my wife tipping a tin of mandarin oranges into a bowl: they had gone all spotty and we decided not to eat them. She put the bowl outside the door and the corgis bolted them down! They were gone in about a minute, after they had fought to see which dog would get them.

8 January 2022

I've told you before that I have the most splendid view from my armchair. Our windowsills are only a foot high so I can see the foreground, which includes our pond and all that goes on there, right up to the big wood that sits on the horizon about two miles away. This wood used to be called Plassey, probably because Clive of India had connections around here. There used to be an acre of a field the other side of the village that was called the Dardenelles. This field was given to the poor of the parish but I don't think they are allowed to call them that now. I had an old man who once worked here who had his history and geography mixed up about this local field, the Dardanelles. He used to tell me that there was once a great battle fought in the Dardenelles field and that the local victors drove the vanquished back all the way to Plassey wood where they massacred them. He never said who the defeated were. I didn't argue with him, he had a good story, why spoil it? If I look at Plassey wood there is a small dip in its shape, against the horizon. This marks a field. Possibly six or seven acres, right in the middle of the wood. I used to buy straw off the man who farmed this field and I had this straw for several years. In the corner of this field was a pile of stones that marked the spot where a cottage had once stood. This has always intrigued me. Why would anyone want to build a cottage in the middle of a wood? What was it like to live there? It was very steep, it would take over an hour to walk to the village. And when I was bringing a load of straw back, I went along the rides in the wood and we used to zig-zag home. The wood is only about two miles away but it used to take two hours to get home safely.

Every year this view is taken from me for about six weeks, because in this window is where our Christmas tree stands. Getting it to stand somewhere else is a bit like trying to stop the tide coming in. This year the tree went up in November and it will stay there until the middle of January. I'm not a fan of Christmas anyway so the trees that go with it don't enthuse me. I used to grow Christmas trees but the last year we grew them, we had a big order cancelled so we took several van loads to an auction 25 miles away. There was a glut of trees that year and after all that, we had to pay to have them taken away by skips!

But help is at hand. One day I am looking at the tree quite closely, in fact I am trying to identify a gap in its branches so I can see beyond it. The tree is an artificial one, we had to stop using a live one because it was up so long it used to shed all its needles. The tree gives a sort of sigh and a curtsey and falls over. The dog, Gomer, is not best pleased because he is sitting on the windowsill. It's a favourite vantage point of his. He likes to sit there and the farm dogs are outside. 'Look at me in the warm and dry'. My wife is not best pleased either because the tree falls on her and on the settee. I get my view back, but only for a couple of hours.

***

'She' is doing some shopping. I don't do shopping so I stay in the car and watch the world go by. We are in our local small town, on the main street. Usually I know most of the people who pass by but today there are lots of strangers about. I decide that they are on holiday in the area for the festive season, which is fair enough. They are quite easy to spot by their dress and behaviour. They wear lots of outdoor clothes, mostly these look new, they are over-dressed, they have hats on and gloves, lots of gloves. Locals don't wear gloves, especially the men. Now here's a strange thing, they always seem to walk on the road, so many of them walk on the road they sometimes stop the traffic. It's quite busy today but clearly it's not as busy as the roads they are used to.

A farmer's wife scurries by but I don't know if I know her, she has a face mask on. I know she is a farmer's wife because she has her husband's wax jacket on and the sleeves are too long. There are other signs as well. There is some cow or sheep poo on the back of it and she has red marks on the backs of her legs where her wellingtons have rubbed.

22 January 2022

We went to the pub on Christmas morning, I've never been to the pub on Christmas day before but there's a first time for everything. I was a bit cautious because there's more covid around here now than ever before, including in our family. My daughter works in the NHS and she made us do a test before we went down to her for our Christmas dinner. We were all clear, still are. The pub was ok but suspect that everyone there was also there the night before, which is the way with pubs.

We go for our Christmas dinner to my daughter's. I supply the turkey. She does about six sorts of vegetables with the meal and puts on quite a show. I ask for someone to pass me the prawn crackers. I don't expect any to be on offer. Not that I need any, there's no room on my plate, but there's everything else. Big mistake. They do have some, they weren't on the table, but there was a big packet in the cupboard. So I had turkey and all the usual trimmings plus some prawn crackers. There's a first time for everything. I only asked for them because it was the only thing I could think of that wasn't on the table already.

I told you some weeks ago that my wife has always wanted me to wear a wedding ring. There was a part of me that for some reason didn't want to wear one, although I have for years worn one of those bracelets with two magnets that are supposed to make me bionic. She would say, 'But so and so wears one,' and I would say, 'So buy him another,' and there would be scowls and that would be the end of that discussion.

But my daughter does a bit of silversmithing and unknown to my wife I ordered a ring off her and it was to be ready for Christmas. When presents were exchanged, the ring made its first appearance. It needed to be made a size bigger but it still didn't get my wife's approval like I thought it would. I thought she would be so pleased that she would pay for it, but she hasn't. My daughter says she will give it me but I suspect I will pay for it sometime. I have shown it to quite a lot of people but my wife now says that I should have had one 40 or 50 years ago. In my experience you can rarely change the past. Apparently this was not the answer she was looking for. It's all been a bit of a disappointment; it hasn't earnt me the marital bonus points I thought it would and it looks as though I will pay for it as well. It could end up in a drawer.

***

We go for a meal in the pub. We take Jane the florist and her husband. It is he that gets our turkey at Christmas so this is our way of paying for it. It is last year's turkey we are paying for now. She is telling us about her flower shop, it's a very small shop so if she isn't busy she is always to be found in the doorway or outside talking to passersby. She is a bit of a character and I always feel that you pay so much for the flowers and so much for the experience. She is telling us that a lot of the people that walk by have dogs on a lead; she likes dogs and always makes a fuss of them. She always has some doggy treats in her pocket and always gives the dog one, on the basis that next time they walk past, the dog drags the owner inside the shop and they invariably buy something.

29 January 2022

If there's one thing I can't do with, it's seeing people on TV, getting their jabs. We see it on every news bulletin. It's not the actual injection I don't like, I couldn't care less about that, in fact I would do it with a sheep vaccinator kit and use the same needle on lots of people and have a big bag of vaccine on my back. No it's not the actual vaccination that bothers me, it's when they put that small piece of cotton wool on to stop it bleeding. I can't bear touching cotton wool and don't even like the sight of it, 'Yuk!' I know people that will leave the room if there are snakes on TV. Heights also do it for me. One year my wife and mother were making mince pies and my father was doing something in the next room. Every half hour he would come in and nick one so she made one with cotton wool inside and he took that. Not amused, but everyone else was.

***

I quite like the mild spells we've been having. I don't like to hear the heating boiler going, that spells cost and we could do without that. There has been a downside, there have been lots of flies about in the house. Big, lazy blue bottles. They are so slow they soon fall prey to a fly swat, which my wife wields with some expertise. She reckons these flies often land on my head but I've never seen one! Our main fly killers are those old-fashioned sticky papers which we mostly hang in the kitchen. We will need some new ones up this week, there's hardly room for a fly to land at present. Who would ever have thought we would still be catching flies in January!

**

My eldest granddaughter is at university and she has a boyfriend who is studying criminology, an industry that will always show growth. He has been sponsored in his final year by the local police authority before joining the force. He is shortly to get some of the bits and pieces that go with joining the police force. Things like handcuffs, a stab vest and police boots. Of course this is right up my street; if I hadn't been a farmer I think I would have joined the police. Not because I have a vocational wish to right wrong but because I'm so nosey. I watch police documentaries endlessly. But it gets better. My granddaughter's boyfriend can't drive so he says that if the police give him a car he will let me drive him about. I've asked him to try and get a 4x4; a BMW X5 would be ok, and I could drive it about the fields in the summer.

My dog Gomer is a big fan of police documentaries as well. He can be very fierce sometimes, especially if Ann or I are about. If we are out of the house, though, then apparently he doesn't get off the settee. If we had burglars he would open the door for them and show them where we kept the silver. Nevertheless he see himself as an Alsatian police dog, never mind that he is a short, fat terrier. For the price of supplying a 4x4 they will get an experienced driver, a police dog and a criminologist all thrown in. Hope they take up the offer.

5 February 2022

Marriage is a finely balanced exercise in give and take. The secret is that when it's your turn to take, if you can do it secretly then it's still your turn, if you follow me. My wife goes off in her car every day to the shop. Just lately she has been asking, 'Is there anything you want?' I know what this is all about, if I need something she can say she had to go shopping for me. So I thought I would turn it to my advantage. I quite fancied some anchovies on toast for my breakfast last week. One of my favourite breakfasts is bacon and laverbread. (Laverbread is the Welsh delicacy of edible seaweed.) So today a tin of laverbread appeared with the anchovies and there was enough for two breakfasts. I like it fried and if you spread it thinly in the pan and crisp it up a bit and serve it with a rasher of bacon, it's really good. But you have to be careful, I wouldn't want anchovies and laverbread every day.

I made the mistake once of saying how much I liked a breakfast cereal so we had a packet on the table for twenty years. Last year I pointed this out and said it would be nice to have some cornflakes for a change: now we don't get either!

We once went for a holiday in Northern Ireland. We went on the ferry to Dublin, we stayed one night in Temple Bar (which most tourists do), and drove on the next day. That day was to be the highlight of our trip because our drive north took us along the spectacular Antrim coast, which must be one of the best drives in the world. At about 4pm the ladies in the back of the car wanted a cup of tea. The best place to get a cup of tea in Ireland is of course in a bar. So the ladies had their cup of tea and the men had a pint each of the dark stuff.

At first we were the only ones in there but we were soon joined by a very big Irishman, he was wearing a suit but he looked as if he would be more at home wearing a high vis jacket and wielding a shovel. I'm a great people watcher but if there's only one person to watch, you end up staring. He spotted me watching him, quite soon. I had seen that he kept dipping in his pocket and taking out some brown stuff and eating it. 'Do you want some of this,' he said. I must confess I did wonder if it was cannabis. 'What is it?' I asked. 'It's dulse.' He said. He could tell that I wasn't any the wiser. 'It's dried seaweed,' he said. So I tried some and we got into conversation. He tells me that there is a lot of this edible seaweed on this northern coast and that people were kept alive by it in the Irish Potato Famine. He tells me that he eats some every day, as does his wife and between them they have 15 children. I am told that I can buy a bag of dulse, should I want to, at any local shop.

Next day I buy a bag to take home. I put some in my pocket the next time I went to the pub and I kept on dipping in my pocket and eating some. Inevitably the questions start, 'What are you eating?' 'Cannabis,' I replied. 'Roger's got some cannabis.' This didn't raise any particular interest. I don't know why I said it, there's always been a lot of drugs in this area. There was a time in the 1960s when there were a lot of hippies around here. They used to get in the pubs, buy a half pint of beer and make it last about three hours. They used to get their pleasure from what they were smoking. Some of them stayed in the area, and some you never saw again.

12 February 2022

I'm not a big fan of the weeks after Christmas. As far as I am concerned it is a time to be endured and only towards the end do you notice any improvements. The days get a bit longer but the land is still too wet for me to have my daily ride around the fields. Usually my next-door neighbour puts some ewes and lambs out very early but I didn't expect to see any this year. Not because he hasn't got any but the storm has left a big oak tree blocking his access to that particular field.

There is quite a lot of that sort of tidying up to do around here. We have a big oak down but it is in the middle of a field so we will leave it until the spring; we will only make a mess if we try to get to it now. But I did see some new lambs yesterday on my way back from the rugby. Quite cheered me up to see them. They were a beacon of light on what was an otherwise gloomy and raw day. For some reason it reminded me of when my son used to play rugby. He used to go off on Saturday and return on Sunday mornings. Rugby matches must have been a lot longer then! He used to arrive home whilst we were having our Sunday breakfast. He would join us and tell us what had gone on in his last 24 hours. The social side of what had gone on was usually more interesting than what had happened on the rugby field.

One day he concluded by saying, 'When I walked down to the club this morning to fetch my car, there was a camel looking over a gate.' My reaction was to think, 'I bet there was.' Then to think, 'If you think you saw a camel perhaps you shouldn't have been driving.' But he was adamant he had seen the camel and we agreed to differ.

The next week I went down to watch the rugby and when I drove home after, there was a camel looking over a gate. The story was that a small local circus family had their winter quarters there and the camel was let out every day to graze and to look over the gate. They have their winter quarters in our parish now and we would often see a Land Rover with a bear sitting in the passenger seat. No seat belt, just sitting there. There's the story of some ramblers once being chased by some escaped baboons, bet they didn't expect that when they started out on their walk!

The local family circus has been in our area for years, my children went to school with their children, I know that the idea of a circus with performing animals is not to most people's taste but we have been living close to them for years and never heard a word of anything but kindness to those animals.

***

It's very easy to forget what our kitchen was like when we came here. There was such a big gap under the door that when it snowed the snow would settle halfway across the floor. Then it was a sort of scullery. I wish we had taken some photographs of it, but taking photographs then was not so easy as it is now. There was a big stone sink and a hand water pump although we soon found out that there was rarely water in the pump. There was one of those cast iron cauldrons that you could light a fire under; this was used to do the washing. There was a big baking oven, also with a fire under it. There was a back staircase to a sitting room and an attic/bedroom where the men who lived in and worked on the farm used to go. In the corner was a row of bells that could be rung by the principals of the house.

Over the first few years all of these were dumped outside. I wish we had kept the bells and still used them. If you were modernising today you would make a feature of all these things but in those days you didn't and they are all gone now. It all sounds a bit Downton Abbey but to be honest it was a tip.

The space in the corner, near the sink, is where our washing machine and dishwasher now sit. There is a big space behind them. This space is very difficult to access. It is where the rodents seem to head on their autumn migration. I used the word rodents, but let's be upfront about this, we don't do B&B anymore, so let's say rats. You get rats in old farmhouses, especially in the autumn when they are looking for somewhere warm and dry to spend the winter. The first sign that we might have rats was when the washing machine and dishwasher started to flood the kitchen. We phone the plumber. He reports that all the pipes have been chewed. He fixes them, but two days later the kitchen is flooded again, the rats have had another chew. This time we fix it in-house, not me but one of my grandsons. I just sit there with my feet on a chair, out of the water, and offer suggestions. This goes down really well. I even suggest that someone should sit in this space all the time, if only to keep the rats out, but this idea is greeted in very much the same way as my other suggestions.

19 February 2022

I shall be glad to see the end of all the endless pro-vegan publicity. It has always intrigued me. I respect the life choices that vegans have taken but they don't seem to respect mine. It's true that I occasionally have a go at vegans, but only when they say that all livestock farming is cruel. They seem to want to convert everyone else, and telling others how to live their lives is very arrogant. They don't understand livestock farming, most of my fields couldn't grow crops that would be ok for human consumption. But they will grow grass and animals live quite well on grass. The grass is converted to milk and meat and humans can consume them. That's how it's always worked. The trick is to give those animals as good a life as you can whilst they are at it.

That's something that they are still to learn elsewhere around the world, places like Australia and New Zealand, where most of your food in the future might come from. If you are a farm animal in Australia or New Zealand, the chances are you will have a hard competitive life.

I think quite a lot about vegans. I have concluded that they quite like being different. And so, if their cause becomes very popular, where will they go next?

Surprise, surprise, the answer is not far away. One advantage to mid-winter that I've not mentioned is that my wife makes a stew or chilli every week, and very good they are too. She is making a stew now and the television is on. It's showing what they call a magazine programme, these are not for me but I don't dare to switch it off. They are interviewing two ladies in San Francisco. I hear the word vegan and so I put my pen down and pay some attention. It turns out that these two ladies are advocating having a love life with the soil. Eco-sexual they call it, I don't have any more details because I suspect this newspaper is read by children and I reached for the remote to switch it off, that's what remotes are for.

***

There's this man I know who, amongst the other things he does, catches moles. He is very good at it. He caught 50 at one farm. He went recently to a 'new' farm, put out about 60 traps, then he went back to the first field where he had started that day and he had caught another 12 whilst he had been there! Of course farmers don't have a vendetta against moles. It's just the mole hills they don't like. If the soil on a mole hill gets into hay or silage, it can spoil it. If sheep or cattle eat the soil it can kill them. It can carry listeria which can be fatal. I've never got over the fact that there aren't any moles in Ireland. It's supposed to be due to a legend concerning Saint Patrick. You would have thought some mischievous person would have released a mole there by now. There's one on my lawn if they want one. I won't tell you how much this man charges per mole because the man who catches mine reads this and he charges less. Sometimes he forgets to charge me if I distract him with a cup of tea. Around here, older people call moles, 'onts'. Therefore a mole hill is an 'onty tump'.

***

My grandson and his partner who live on the farm, have two dogs. One is a Labrador and one is a collie, a sort of farm dog. I don't think anyone ever told him he was a farm dog because I have yet to see him doing anything that is remotely useful on a farm. I think the Lab is too thin but that could be because he is young and still growing, as opposed to my dog Gomer who is so fat he would make a good coffee table. Now here's a strange thing. When they go out they take the two dogs with them. Farm dogs don't usually go out like that. Farm dogs are supposed to stay at home whilst you are away and keep an eye on things. They are supposed to hang about the yard and come instantly if you should return home and call them. It was strange to see the dogs both down watching the rugby on Saturday. The farm dog can't believe his luck, he was on a lead and it seemed strange to see a collie on a lead amongst the other dogs there, all popular breeds and fashionable crosses. The Lab had a coat on, the collie didn't, I don't know what that was about. Perhaps it was a class thing, Labs can be very snobbish.

26 February 2022

How on earth did they find a plane to rescue all those dogs from Kabul? To me, and to most of the watching world, slots for planes to land at Kabul were at a premium, as were planes themselves. If it was possible to fill a plane with dogs and cats, it would have been easier to fill it with people. Who made the decision? The images from Afghanistan ever since have been dire. Starving children, children walking bare foot in the snow, people selling their children in order to buy scraps of food. You would need to be very influential to get away with prioritising dogs and cats, so who was it? Someone, somewhere with a lot of influence made that choice and as a nation we should be ashamed. I know that it wouldn't make much difference in the whole scheme of things but if there are people about who can make that sort of decision, surely we deserve to know who they are? The watching world probably think it was disgraceful and I agree with them.

***

I can't do with the dog staring at me in the evenings any longer. He sits about two yards in front of my armchair and just stares, no blinking, just stares. When my wife goes shopping on Thursdays she mostly buys me some fruit, and lately it's been some grapes. I eat a bit on most evenings. The trouble is that the dog, Gomer, just loves fruit. It doesn't matter what sort of fruit it is, he will eat it. And there lies the problem. Apparently you are not supposed to give dogs any fruit, I am told it might kill them. So on the evenings I don't have any fruit he doesn't believe me and that's why we get the staring. I usually give him three grapes, he prefers the black ones, I know I shouldn't but thus far he has come to no harm. If you had to endure such a plaintive stare, I'm sure you would give him three grapes as well.

Now here's a strange thing, when I was a boy my mother used to have a little white mongrel bitch. You rarely hear the word mongrel these days, but all these crossbred, expensive puppies are just mongrels really. Anyway this little mongrel had a love for blackberries. Just as they became ripe she would spend from dawn to dusk around the hedgerows eating blackberries. She would carefully pick them with her teeth and just as carefully eat them. When she was on her second go around she would pick the higher ones by standing on her back legs, carefully making sure that she didn't get prickled. She must have eaten tons of them, and they didn't do her any harm.

She was almost all white and when she finally came home in the evenings she would have a purple head and neck where she had spilled some juice. There's always plenty of blackberries locally down the banks of some lakes. There's a saying that you should never eat the lower ones, just in case the fishermen have peed on them.

***

There is rarely something new in farming. Very often a new idea is not a new idea at all, it's just an old idea that has new technologies applied to it. There are fashions in farming, a latest one is not to plough arable land and to drill this year's crop into the stubble of last year's. There are plenty of drills that will do this but thirty years ago lots of farmers had a drill that would do just the same, and they all ended up parked in the nettles. My neighbour had one of these drills parked in an orchard, which was a sort of graveyard for machines he no longer used. One year he had about ten billy goats there to keep the orchard tidy and they used to love climbing onto the hopper of this drill. It was a fine sight to see all these billy goats on top of this drill, silhouetted against the sun as they waited to greet the new day.

I used to have a saying that said that if you farmed the same way for thirty years, for ten years you would be a sort of slowcoach, behind with how things were being done. For ten years you would be the same as everyone else. But, not to worry, for the next ten years you would be ahead, a sort of pioneer.

Farmers get lots of magazines to read and I confess I sort of scan read them and only read articles or items in which I have an interest. A short piece caught my eye recently. It concerned the feeding of gorse to cattle. I suspect that to make gorse an ingredient for a cattle mix they would mill it, and that some new milling technique had made this viable.

But just returning to the theme of nothing new in farming, do you remember that they used to feed gorse to cattle in the book *Lorna Doone*? It's true that they called gorse 'furze' then but it's always fascinated me – off-hand I can't think of a less likely feeding stuff than gorse! Just how hungry would cattle have to be to eat it – all those prickles! There was no mention of milling it in those days so it might have been a way of just keeping cattle alive until the grass came in the spring. The cattle they didn't want to keep were probably slaughtered in the autumn and put in barrels of salt: they were the lucky cows who didn't have to eat gorse to stay alive.

5 March 2022

For 12 months I've had trouble with my mobile phone. The phone I had needed replacing and since then I've had three new ones and they haven't worked well. This is a bad area for phone signals. I can get a signal if I drive up to my top field because the mast is in the next field but who wants to do that in the winter? I get texts ok but I've not had a phone call for weeks. I carry the phone in case of an emergency but my life is ok without any calls. Mobile phones have become a fashion accessory, a bit like a bottle of water, but life without one is ok. Strange but true.

***

There's a robin lives outside our kitchen door. He's getting very cheeky. If the door is open, he flies in, he does this two or three times a day. Trouble is he's not always good at flying out again. We mostly have to catch him, which is not easy. It's bad enough now because it is winter and the door is mostly closed, but in the summer the door is invariably open and we have one of these 'stable' door arrangements where the top half is always open. It's a bit of a novelty, having a tame robin in the kitchen but if I wanted a bird in the kitchen I would probably get a parrot in a cage. I would teach him lots of bad language if only I knew some.

***

Like most farmers, I take a weekly farming magazine. There are only two real national publications and I take one of those. Years ago there was a publication called the *Farmer and Stock Breeder* but that was amalgamated (which is another word for swallowed up) by one of the others. You still get farmers of a certain age referring to one of the present-day magazines as *The Stockbreeder* which is quite remarkable because it disappeared 40 or 50 years ago! My favourite feature in the magazine I take is of old photographs that readers send in. They are often a group, mostly a family, standing around a prize-winning animal that has just come out top of its class somewhere. All the humans are in their best clothes, polished gaiters and stiff collars. They are invariably standing self-consciously – having your photo taken was probably a big deal then. Sometimes they are of farming activities like hay making and shearing or threshing and it is always interesting to see how things have changed. It's interesting to see how the dogs have changed. I note that if there's some heavy repetitive work about, there are always some women in the photos but women rarely make it onto the photos of prize winning beasts!

I just love old farming photos that show the farming activities of yesteryear. I've got a book of old rural photographs somewhere, but like a lot of things in my life, I haven't a clue where it is. My two favourite photos are one of a line of horses making their way to a day's work on an arable farm. The horses are all in the pairs that they will work in, and they are being ridden by the men whose job it is to work them. There are several pairs of horses in the line, something like five pairs. The pride on the faces of those horsemen is only matched by the shine of the harness that the horses are wearing.

The other photo shows several teams of horses and their horsemen drawn up at the top of a big ploughed field. They are all having their bait. The horses all have their nosebags on and the men are all sitting down on the bank at the edge of the field eating their sandwiches, probably bread and cheese. There is so much in the photograph you could almost write a story about it.

Before corn was cut by combines, it used to be cut by a binder. A binder produced sheaves. These were put in to stooks ie they were stood up in groups. I came in as a schoolboy just as combines were coming in and I did several fields the old way, stacking sheaves. You had to do it tidy, as standing in stooks was part of the ripening process. Especially oats, there used to be a saying that you should stook the oats and then go to chapel three times before you carted them. Stooking sheaves was a good companionable activity, unless there were thistles amongst the corn, which would play hell with your forearms!

Here's a question for somebody. A binder which cut the corn always cut on the left but mowers even today, always cut on the right, why? I've asked this question of vintage farm machinery enthusiasts and they don't have an answer. Before too long there won't be anyone alive to ask because, like the horsemen before them, anyone who used a binder will have passed on.

12 March 2022

There's been a lot of news about this week, there's been a lot of wind as well. It seems we can't do anything about the news and we know we can't do anything about the wind. It seems the hard times are a-coming. If, like me you have to put fuel in the car, top up the heating oil or buy red diesel for the tractor, you don't need a good memory to recall how much these items cost you 12 months ago. Our cow cake has gone up about £100 a ton over the last months and we are getting less for our milk than we were four years go. That can't last. I thought that selling organic milk would be a good place to be but it isn't. No one owes me a living but neither do I owe anyone impossibly cheap milk.

***

I don't usually mention this, but a few years ago I received an honour. I told my immediate family but I've never told anyone else and I've never written it down. Secretly I'm very proud of it and any 'cash for honours' seems to only undermine that pride. But like most things in my life, it all has its humorous side. I didn't know anything about it, still don't. But I remember getting home from a three-day break in the early evening. There was a pile of post on the kitchen table and I went through it. I didn't open any, mind, I never do. I usually know what every letter contains and it's usually a bill. Halfway through I find this letter from the Lord Chancellor's department and assume it's because I haven't paid a bill. It's a bit annoying because I always pay bills before that happens but I put it, unopened, with all the other letters. But I remember being curious and extracting it from the pile. Do I open it now or shall I leave it for the morning? Curiosity gets the better of me, but it nearly went in the bin.

***

We've got this friend who comes here on one morning a week to help with the housework. She arrives just before breakfast and her first job is to make herself a cup of coffee and me a cup of tea. She always sniffs the milk when she gets it out of the fridge, I wish she wouldn't do that, it puts doubt in your mind when you shouldn't have any. I don't know if she has this habit because she's had some bad experiences, but our milk is always ok.

Then she sits down for a chat. Today she is telling me about when she used to help out in a care home. She used to tidy the room of an old man who always did the crossword in the local paper. He always did it in front of her and she couldn't get over how quickly he did it. It wasn't a cryptic crossword, it was in the local paper and they called it the quick crossword. She did it herself but it always took her about twenty minutes. This man did it in about three, she was full of admiration for him, he was so quick his pen hardly left the paper. She used to think 'fair play, his mind is still as sharp as ever.' One day she was at work and he wasn't in his room but the newspaper was open at the crossword.

So she thought she would have a look. What he'd written was just meaningless, in fact there was no connection between what he'd written and the clues. Yet he had this reputation throughout the home that he was so astute he could do a crossword quicker than anyone else. There was no harm in it, we all need a bit of fantasy within our lives.

I used to fantasise that I would like to ride on a horse up the main street of our local town, dressed as Clint Eastwood in the film *The Outlaw Josey Wales*. But I don't fantasise about that anymore, I'd be afraid of falling off the horse, I'm too old to fall off anything.

I think of this lady who helps with our housework as the 'dog lady'. She surely qualifies for that description because she had five dogs. She takes them for a walk twice a day. She has a dog that sometimes refuses to get out of the truck and once stayed there for three days. I've never seen her dogs but I think three of them are Alsatians. She once showed me a photo of the dog that won't get out of the truck – it was all attitude and teeth. Get too close and you could lose a hand.

19 March 2022

Years ago I used to sell game into France. Our season used to start in August, with the grouse, and proceed through the seasons until we finished at the end of January. Shot pheasant was the main item we handled and in November, when shooting was at its height, we used to turn round 10,000 a week. We ran a collection service so I used to travel hundreds of miles in my van. I had company on my journeys, I used to employ a man called Jack who was on his pension. About twice a week we would have big days collecting. We would travel to our furthest shoot, which might be 150 miles away and we would aim to be there by 8am and we would then work our way home calling at various shoots along the way. It meant early starts, often at 3 or 4 o'clock in the morning and I would collect Jack at a point close to where he lived.

In all the years we did this I can never remember Jack being late or in a bad mood. He always called me partner but then he called most people partner. If we were on one of our long journeys he would always have a bag with him and as he got in he always used to say, 'Got two costrels today partner, we've got a long way to go.' This was referring to the two thermos flasks he was carrying. One had some very sweet tea in it and the other had sweet tea plus some whiskey. He would serve me a cup of tea but on the way home he would say, 'Time to break out the number two costrel now.' I only had one cup because I was driving but Jack would soon drink it all. I used to ask him why he called it a costrel. He had worked on a farm when he was younger and he said that they used to hang a small barrel under the harvest wagons. They would fill this barrel with cider and they would always empty the barrel before they went home; it was apparently bad luck to take cider home. They always used to call this barrel a costrel.

I thought no more about it until one day I was at the Welsh Folk Museum at St Fagans which is just to the west of Cardiff. It's well worth a visit if you can manage it, not least because they have reconstructed a lot of buildings as they once were. For example, there is a row of miner's cottages, re-erected and furnished. And there is a farming section and in it is a wagon that would have been used to carry hay and sheaves and under this wagon, slung on chains, was a little barrel that carried a sign that said, 'costrel'.

After the war, where Jack had been a paratrooper at Arnhem, he was a lorry driver. His two main jobs had been to take pit props to the mines and to take foam rubber from South Wales to Glasgow. He often used to tell me that after you had been through the traffic lights at Monmouth, you could drive all the way to Glasgow without any restriction. He often used to say that you needed to plan your journey so that you never left your lorry parked up overnight in Glasgow, because you would never know if it would be there next day.

If you were to ask Jack his background he would probably say that he was 100% English and yet here he was using a Welsh word most days without knowing it! Many of the farming families around here came out of Wales 100 years ago in the recession of the 1920s. I've known families where their grandparents never spoke English.

Now here's a story. I used to be involved in a milk cooperative and every year we had quite a big stand at the Royal Welsh Show. I used to go to the show for four days. One afternoon it was very wet and outside, on the avenue, a reporter for the Welsh language television service was interviewing a boy of about ten years old. There was the reporter, the cameraman, the boy and his parents. Because it was so wet and because they were having such difficulty I suggested to the reporter that they conduct the interview on our stand, which would give them some shelter. She gladly said yes and I thought no more of it. When they had finished and gone their separate ways, she, the reporter came to thank me. She said that the boy had won an essay prize in the Welsh language and she had been interviewing him in Welsh.

When the interview had finished, the parents told her that the family had only been living in Wales for eight months and that their son went to a Welsh language primary school because it was the nearest. That before they had moved to Wales he had lived all his life in north Derbyshire. The reporter told me that all the time she was interviewing the lad she never picked up, by his pronunciation or his accent, that he was a Welsh learner and if the parents hadn't told her their story she would never have guessed. All that is a far cry from the days when children were physically punished if they were heard to use the Welsh language in school.

26 March 2022

Who remembers the hard winter of 1963? My wife reckons it is usual for me to spend a whole evening without speaking, so it is her that makes the first comment. 'During that freeze I used to walk two miles in the snow to post you a letter.' She obviously expects a reply but we could be on dangerous ground here so I need to be careful. I stop to think. The best I can come up with is, 'Would you do it now?' No reply, but it's still my turn. 'You must have known you were onto a good thing.' This goes down really well, as you can imagine.

But I have my own memories of that particular winter. I was looking after a herd of cows at the other side of the village. It wasn't that far but it used to take me 45 minutes to walk there and I did it for a month. I had to finish milking by 7 o'clock in the morning because the electric would lose power at 7 o'clock and you could hear the vacuum pump getting slower and slower. They reckoned that 7 o'clock was the time when kettles were switched on all over Cardiff and the demand exceed supply. I don't remember what time I started out, it must have been 4 o'clock. I remember being very pragmatic, 'I won't let this beat me.'

Strangely, the most frustrating aspect in that winter was when things got a bit better. Roads were now passable, even if they were only single track, and I could get to work in my van. The trouble was that there was a very steep hill to negotiate on the way home. You could only get up this hill if you built up some speed, some momentum, on the flat before the hill. The steepest part of the hill was the last bit and time after time I would be halted by other vehicles that had got stuck. The trick was to back onto the flat piece before you started the climb but a lot of drivers hadn't worked this out.

A lot of people can't drive on snow, a problem we still have in rural areas today. Never mind reversing! One lunchtime I set off home at 1 o'clock and I was still on the hill at two! I turned around and went to milk: you had to be finished by five. 5 o'clock was when the people of Cardiff started to cook their tea!

The most dangerous job that winter was giving the cows some water. I can remember that we manged to keep one tap running all the time and we gave the cows a drink twice a day. This doesn't sound very much but believe me, they were very difficult times. We used to fill a tank for the cows with a hosepipe and they were so thirsty that it was a bit scary when they were all fighting to have a drink.

Jack, my companion in the van when we were delivering game years later, was once driving in some deep snow with me. He was reminiscing and I was concentrating because if I got stuck I'd never hear the last of it. He was telling me of a winter, I can't remember if it was 1963 or 1947, the snow was so deep that local men couldn't get to work in the woods. I think it must have been 1947 because he was taking a load of pit props to the mine every day, so if the men couldn't get to work in the woods, they couldn't cut him a load of pit props and he couldn't get his lorry into the woods anyway!

Anyway 'they' put a gang of local men to clear the road to a valley that had been cut off for some time. It was approached by a sunken lane and the snow had blown off the fields and filled the lane in. The men had only shovels and wheelbarrows to work with; there wasn't the kit about in those days.

Jack was telling me that the snow was so deep that when the men got a bit of a sweat on they took their jackets off and hung them on the electric wires. I didn't reply because at the time I was crashing the van through a snowdrift, where the snow had blown through a gateway. I think that Jack took my silence to be disbelief, and I remember that he gave me a hard look, which was unusual for Jack.

The next time he was working with me he produced a black and white photograph, it showed about twenty men, with shovels, clearing snowdrifts and they did indeed have their jackets folded up and put on the electric wires. The wires were about as high up as the snow and they weren't sagged down. Can you imagine getting a gang of men to do that sort of work today? No, I can't either.

Here's a Jack story to finish. We regularly used to pass a pub that was advertising steak and chips for £2.50. To put this into context it was at a time when most pubs were charging £10 for the same thing. 'I took the missus there for that the other night,' says Jack. 'What was it like?' I ask. There's a long silence then Jack says, '£2.50 was plenty of money for it.'

2 April 2022

We hear a lot about the rising cost of food. It isn't rising for me because we are getting just a bit less for our milk than we were four years ago. No, I can't work it out either. I take a keen interest in what things cost. So when my wife is preparing my breakfast, I'm always asking what items cost. I usually have an egg on toast for breakfast and usually there are baked beans or tinned tomatoes as well. When the tin appears I always ask what it cost. It is clear to me that the well-known brands are usually twice the price of the own-label products. There is rarely anything to choose between them on quality, they probably come out of the same factory, so there is a saving to be had there.

We have a farm secretary calls here every two weeks for half a day. She always has her lunch here and she just loves a certain brand of chocolate bar. I'm certain that these are half the size that they were a few years ago, they are certainly smaller. That is an increase in price, whatever way you look at it, even if it's more devious!

It's a funny old thing but most days she, my wife, has started doing me a pudding with my meal at night, what's all that about? She can't avoid it because she calls to see the florist on Thursdays and there is always a box waiting for her on the counter. There is always a fruit pie in the box. But not to argue about what's in the box, just take it and do as you are told. If she runs out of fruit pie she does me a tin of rice pudding. I just love rice pudding. It's just the same as baked beans and tinned tomatoes, the brand is double the price of the own label but the own label is just as good. The only trouble with tinned rice pudding, warmed up in a microwave, is that you rarely get the skin on it that you get with a homemade pudding. Skin on a rice pudding! Yum! A spoonful of jam as well? Yum Yum!

Yesterday afternoon I went down to watch the local rugby. I was only gone 2-3 hours but at the garage I passed, the fuel had gone up 3p in the time. I can remember the days when we used to take a can of diesel down the fields if we had some rubbish to burn. If there was some diesel left we used to put it on the fire so that we didn't have to carry it back. We don't do that anymore.

***

One of the things I remember from my childhood is that my father would follow you about the house making sure you had not left an electric fire on. We had built-in electric fires in our bedrooms but he had taken the plugs off so we couldn't use them. The trick was to get into the kitchen, where the fire went all night, just as quickly as you could. We often had frost inside our bedroom windows, still do in fact, there's progress for you! If we had a bath, which we sometimes did, we needed to switch the immersion heater on to boost the temperature of the water. But if you forgot to switch it off you were in serious trouble!

Later in his life, retired and in a different house, Dad now had central heating. He just loved that. He said, often, that if you had central heating you should be able to sit about in your shirt sleeves. Which he did. I'm writing this in our kitchen, the only heat in here comes from our old Rayburn. It's dead today, there's a man coming soon to fit a new wick. It's 13 degrees in here now I don't find it cold but most people would. There's such a lot of energy wasted. If you watch television, especially the news, there's always people in the background going about in their shirts and thin dresses. If I was in charge I would turn the thermostat down a couple of degrees and make everyone wear a jacket or a pullover. Why are all these churches lit up at night? There's very few people there at 10 o'clock on Sunday mornings, I don't expect there's many there at 10 o'clock on a Friday night. My Dad came from a generation that didn't waste anything. They didn't waste anything because when they were growing up they couldn't afford to, it was a way of life that we would do well to emulate. And they had to live through the stringency of two World Wars.

Just as an example, thousands of dogs and cats disappeared in the early years of the Second World War. Just imagine the outcry that would greet such a measure today! The simple truth was that there just wasn't enough food about to feed dogs and cats. My own parents were given a Samoyed puppy, (a big white fluffy dog), as a wedding present. It was on their early photos and then it disappeared, I often wondered what happened to it. I wish I'd asked them, I can't ask them now.

9 April 2022

At some sort of signal, which I am yet to understand, about twenty Canada geese drop down in the field in front of our house. They are here to claim the tiny nesting site on our pond. They do the same every year, but this year seemed to be more violent. There's no way of telling if some of them came here last year, if their number includes the pair that nested here last year or perhaps some of their progeny. One Canada goose is very much like another. They fought all day and it was serious and noisy fighting. By next morning, order was restored. There were only two left. The goose was on the nest site, making herself comfortable on last year's nest and the gander, making himself tall and erect, was out of the grass.

There's more spring drama outside our back door. The huge colony of sparrows that used to inhabit the creepers there are still missing: maybe a dozen at most now. The only difference I can detect is an aggressive robin. If you are a sparrow you can have a hard time from a robin. I'll keep you posted.

***

I remember reading somewhere that dogs spend 80% of their time asleep. I expect that the 80% is an average figure and some dogs like my Gomer are in the high nineties. He spends most of his life asleep on our settee. He sleeps on his back, with all his bits on show. He drags himself to the kitchen at meal times in case we drop some food on the floor, which he quickly hoovers up. His most active time is in the evening when he is about, watching us watch the TV or read the newspapers. He's doing it now, staring at me. He will stare at me for ages, never a blink, and he will stare for an hour without moving. There had to be a reason for it, and now I think I have the answer. His favourite toy is a small rugby ball. He just loves chasing this. It used to have a squeak when he first bit it but he soon finished that off! So we throw it and he goes to fetch it back. We would do it again but he never brings it back to where we can reach it. He hasn't worked that bit out yet. I say that he is too thick to bring it back properly. It is a long way to get out of your armchair to retrieve a ball that is 10 feet away. So he sits there and stares at you, hoping you will get up and throw the ball. If he would only drop it at your feet, you would.

Anyway, he's feeling a bit full of himself at the moment. Yesterday he caught and killed a mouse in our kitchen. It wasn't a very quick mouse, in fact it had all the characteristics of a mouse that had eaten some poison. It had been about our kitchen for about an hour. It had crossed the floor several times. Gomer was bred to catch rodents. I even fancied catching it myself if it came any nearer and I was bred to take it easy. This particular mouse made the mistake of hiding behind the Rayburn but it left its tail sticking out. And Gomer had it. Now there's a warrior in his demeanour and his shoulders have a squareness to them.

16 April 2022

I used to do quite a lot of after dinner speaking. I was never an ad lib speaker, I used to have it all written down, word for word, on some cards and I couldn't vary my speech after I had started it. I was very nervous and that was my way of coping with it. You might wonder why I volunteered to speak if I was so nervous but I have always believed that you should stretch yourself. One year I did 34 dinners but that is too much and it threatens to take over your life. I never used to tell jokes, something I learnt the hard way. I used to try to amuse the audience but by telling them stories instead. One year I was given a Jethro CD for Christmas. I thought it was really funny so I decided to use most of the jokes in a speech I was doing in Exeter in January. The man who introduced me took twenty minutes and told most of the jokes I had laboriously written down! So I had to scan my memory for stories and do the best I could. It was one of life's lessons and I shall never forget it! Anyway, here's a joke, some of you will have heard it before but there will be some of you who haven't. There's this farmer with a terminal illness, he suspects it's terminal but he's not been told yet. So he goes to the doctor and puts a lot of pressure on him and eventually the doctor agrees that he is going to die. But that isn't the end of it. 'Give it straight to me, how long have I got?' The doctor doesn't want to commit himself but the farmer is insistent so in the end the doctor says, 'If I was you I wouldn't buy any green bananas.' Get it? Then there was the time when I went to speak in Dorset. My host gave me such a large gin and tonic before we left for the dinner that when I got up to speak I dropped all my cards on the floor and I had to wing it. I'm trying to forget about that!

***

Since I lost my sister it's even more of a reminder to my brother and I that we should make even more of an effort to keep in touch. He lives about two hours drive away but if we both drive an hour towards each other it's no big deal and we can meet for lunch. He had grandchildren that I don't know and vice versa so I will include them in future. If you don't know your relations well, that's how families drift apart and I will have a good try to see that that doesn't happen. Yesterday was my birthday, not a big birthday, but a good enough reason to meet for lunch. There were only three of us but I will try to get some of my grandchildren there as well next time. The place where we meet has changed hands and now you can get a good curry there as well. That's an added reason why we should go.

Most of the conversation centres around memories, as you can imagine, and one of these is as follows. When I was first married and my brother was single and a student, he and a good friend came to stay with us. This particular day had been spent on essential farming activities such as shooting rats with my airgun. I can't remember why but we were all going out that evening and there was a certain urgency to getting ready.

We didn't have a shower in those days, we had a big cast iron bath. It was huge and you could lie full length in it. We were to swop it for a green plastic one, the same as everyone else.

Big mistake. I can remember carrying it downstairs on my own because the builders bet me I couldn't. I knew they were winding me up and they didn't want to carry it themselves but I wasn't about to let a group of builders beat me! So we are waiting to go out. My brother was last to use the bathroom and he seemed to take ages. With hindsight I can't blame him, there was plenty of hot water and he must have been enjoying the lie out, full length. I went from being impatient to very tetchy. 'I'll shift him,' I remember saying. I went outside and fetched a dead rat that we had shot earlier in the day, I didn't fetch any old rat I fetched the biggest I could find. I carried it gingerly by its tail, upstairs and into the bathroom. My brother was lying out full length in the bath, he seemed surprised to see me. I tossed the dead rat between his legs. Off-hand I don't think I've ever seen anything move quicker. It worked ok. I can't remember what happened to the rat, I think we sent it down the toilet, and I can remember that next day I was ordered to fit a lock inside the bathroom door.

23 April 2022

It must be for three or four years now that I have been receiving texts from a major trade union. During that time I have been asked to vote in elections, go on strike and generally support union activity. I am sure that one text addressed me as a local representative! On my phone there was an option to stop all these messages and I did try that, but it didn't work. These messages are not meant for me and there is an element of eavesdropping involved. But now they are a part of my life, sometimes I don't get a text for a month sometimes I get two or three in a week. I don't feel guilty, after all I didn't start them. So I am driving back from a meeting my brother for my birthday lunch, and my phone, which I always carry in my shirt breast pocket, gives a whisper and a bit of a twitch which tells me that a new text has arrived.

'They' have got me a new mobile phone. It's got one of these touch screens, like everyone else has got, but I haven't a clue how to use it. I don't know how to make a call or how to send a text, in fact all it does is receive texts but my life goes on regardless. I've been at home about an hour when I remember that I have a text that I've not read. It's from the trade union and it's to wish me a happy birthday. I delete it and think no more about it. Then an hour later I have second thoughts. How do they know when my birthday is! What else do they know? It's all a bit scary isn't it? In no time at all it's gone from a bit of a laugh to an issue, probably time to press a button and stop it all. But if they know when my birthday is, what do other organisations know?

***

As long as I can remember, if we have had scraps of food left over they have been thrown out of our back door. They were never there for long. If it was crusts, for example, they were just thrown; if there was some spare gravy the crusts would be put in a bowl and the gravy tipped on top. We assumed that the gravy would soften the crusts and thus make it all more palatable. The food scraps would soon disappear inside the sparrows that always lived in the creepers outside our back door. I don't know what the collective noun for sparrows is so I will make one up. A tumult of sparrows. It sounds about the right name for perhaps a hundred sparrows we can see eating some food scraps.

But all that has changed. There are only about ten sparrows there now, possibly due to the presence of that very cheeky robin I had mentioned earlier. This robin comes into our kitchen at every opportunity but it's better now than it was because he now finds his own way back out again. He's not been on our kitchen table yet but I can see he's thinking about it. He has been named George. Years ago we had a homing pigeon up the yard; he was there for about six months, he was also called George. Until one day he went inside a cat. But here's a very strange thing.

When we have scraps and we put them in a bowl outside, the robin, George, eats them alongside Gomer my dog. It's quite a strange sight to see these two sharing a bowl, neither of them seems to mind at all. There's no doubt who is in charge. When they get down to the last morsel, Gomer gets a sharp peck on the nose and so he retreats. I wonder why the robin doesn't mind sharing with the dog but not with the sparrows which are chased off relentlessly. One of life's little quirks.

30 April 2022

When does a dairy farmer stop being a dairy farmer? When he stops selling milk. If you use that criteria I am no longer a dairy farmer. Let me explain. Most of the land we farm was on a short-term lease. It was called a Farm Business Tenancy. We had it for ten years to start with and we had an arrangement to keep it for five years when we converted to organic but overall I expect we had it for twenty years. It was 215 acres. We have always known that it was a short term arrangement but the land becomes a part of your life and you treat it as well as you can.

The last month has been as traumatic as I can remember, as we have been told to quit the land next March. No reason, no explanation, just a red card. And it gets complicated. Our dairy cows were clear of TB and saleable. Ideally we would have liked to keep them until next year but in that time they would be subject to two more TB tests and if there was a failure (which I fully expected) they would be more difficult to sell. So most of the cows are gone, there's only a few stragglers left and some young cattle.

I intend to enjoy that land for the next year. It is there I see the most spectacular views and of course, 'my hares'. We, as a family, are quite pragmatic about it now, there's nothing to be done but we are not sure there is a living to be had on the land we have left. We have bought a milk dispensing machine and we will install that in a local shop.

If we are annoyed, and we sometimes are, it is because since we went organic, it has become a perfect picture of what a farm should look like, especially when the clovers are in flower. The previous tenants were into continuous cereals, for years and years, but we have carted manure there for twenty years and now it is looking so well. Someone else will get the benefit but at least we did it.

***

Every Sunday morning we go to see our daughter. We go at about 10 o'clock and it's usually a quiet ride, as there are not many cars about. I remember stopping for fuel one day and I said to the girl at the garage, 'It's quiet this morning,' and she said, 'That's because lots of people do not get out of bed before 10am on Sundays, they have a cup of coffee and then they get the car out, so by 11am the roads will be really busy.' But it's busier this particular morning. We have only gone a few hundred yards when we meet a long line of cars. They are all old cars, vintage cars, probably on their way to a rally or show. They are mostly from the 1950s and 60s which means I remember most of them, unfortunately, but I quite enjoy seeing them.

About two miles further on they are preparing for the finish of a cycle race. It must be an important race because there's lots of people about. They are putting up bollards and signs to show where the finishing line is. We have to go through one of our local small towns and we stop at a garage to get our Sunday papers. The garage is full of motorcycles and half of them seem to be revving up and making a noise. When the riders take their helmets off I can see that they are mostly middle-aged men who are riding the big bikes they probably couldn't afford when they were younger. Two or three of them will probably be killed before we get to the autumn, it's the same everywhere, middle aged men, big bikes and sharp corners!

Years ago a friend of mine was taking his daughter and her pony to a gymkhana and he met a line of bikes at a sharp corner. He said that the first two or three were ok, the next two or three were on the white line and the last one was over the white line but had committed to the line he was to take. He went under the horse box and died!

When we retrace our steps a couple of hours later, all the motorbikes are gone. Local rumour suggests that they get a car park ticket with the time on it and then they go to the seaside and get another ticket so they can see how long it took. It's a journey of about 70 miles. Strictly speaking it isn't a race, but it is, isn't it?

The finish of the cycle race is now awash with people. There's a part of me that resents their presence. Part of the attraction of a lovely area like this is it's peace and tranquillity and they are spoiling that. I don't like how they walk, unhurriedly, in the middle of the road as if they owned it. I don't like how every gateway is blocked with cars. It's never crossed their minds that someone might want to get in that field! So I see them as an intrusion. Am I becoming a miserable old sod?

7 May 2022

Panic! Our robin, George, disappeared for 48 hours. For two days he wasn't outside our kitchen door. He usually appears as soon as he hears the door open. The sparrows have enjoyed this new-found freedom and there have been up to twenty eating the scraps. Then after two days he reappears, no explanation, and he soon re-establishes the pecking order with him at the top. I wonder where he's been? Wherever it was it's done him no harm as he is immediately back to his normal cheeky self. It's been good on the bird front lately. I've seen some lapwings on this farm which I hadn't seen for about twenty years. There was a flock of about twenty on the land we rent but I haven't seen them for a couple of weeks now. Possibly they are the same birds, there's no way of telling. I'm just glad to see them.

**

We have mice in our kitchen. This is unusual at this time of year. Usually rodents are going outside for the summer. Some of the mice are quite big and these are called rats. I have been hearing them run about in the attic above our kitchen for about a week now. If someone else heard them I always used to say it was the hot water pipes rattling. Proof eventually turned up because they were carrying big dog biscuits from Gomer's bowl and putting them in one of the drawers of our kitchen units. I've no idea how they got them there but you have to admire their industry. My son has put some rat poison in the attic and I haven't heard them this morning. Apparently, having rats is all my fault but I've been accused of worse things.

**

My daughter has a grassy yard next to some redundant buildings, where she keeps her hens. That's why I have egg on toast for breakfast most days. 12 months or so ago these hens were joined by a turkey stag. He's been there so long he probably thinks he's a hen as well, but then what do I know? He's a wild turkey stag, he's been about the woods and fields for some time before he moved in with the hens. His name is Boris; if you have noticed, most turkey stags round here end up being called Boris. Boris isn't at all aggressive, which is unusual for a stag turkey. I used to have a pack of turkeys and they were led by a Boris. They used to stop our neighbours leaving their houses to go to work or school in the mornings and stop them getting back in to their houses at the other end of day. They got so nasty in the end I had to banish them to a wood miles away and even then they would walk half a mile to a lane where they used to stop the traffic. I think that the Boris we are talking about now is what they call a North American turkey. Years ago most of the shoots around here used to rear some. They are more athletic than the sort of turkey that you eat at Christmas and they used to fly over the guns with the pheasants on shooting days. I don't shoot anymore and had not given the matter much thought but I did mention it to a late friend of mine who used to do a fair bit of shooting. He was never one to mince his words and he replied. 'Shooting at turkeys is —— —— cruel.' He went on to explain that shooters that were expecting to shoot pheasants only carried light shot, shot that would rarely bring down a turkey. He went on to explain that even so 'the guns' couldn't resist a pot shot at a turkey, in fact that they did it with some glee. 'I had to tell some of them off,' he said. (I wouldn't like to be on the wrong end of that.) The truth of the story is that most of the turkeys made it to the safety of the woods but on the way they might have picked up lots of wounds from light shot that would hurt them but not bring them down. Once in the safety of the woods they would either get better or die a slow painful death. I suspect it is for this reason that I've not heard of any shoots rearing flying turkeys for a long time. Like most things in life, you have to think of the consequences.

I miss having turkeys about the yard. We once had a neighbour we didn't much like and he had a couple of boats in his garden, (which is as far as they ever went!) Our turkeys used to perch on these boats at night and leave a line of turkey poo underneath, but the neighbour was too afraid of them to chase them off.

14 May 2022

Last week I wrote about shooting turkeys, or rather why you shouldn't. Whilst I am at it I am not sure you should shoot at mallard either. A duck drive, at the start of the day, is the mainstay of many a commercial shoot. The trouble is that of all the game birds, the mallard gets used to humans very quickly and soon becomes tame. I remember one shoot where they reared a lot of duck but when shooting started they used to feed them on a lake about 400 yards away. The idea was that the ducks would fly back over the guns to their place of refuge. That's how most shooting works.

The trouble was that the ducks soon worked out that if they walked back, they wouldn't be shot at! So the guns would be spread out to do some shooting and all these ducks, hundreds of them, would be walking back amongst them, safe in the knowledge that if they stayed on the ground they wouldn't be shot at.

So desperate was the person who ran the shoot to get the ducks to fly that he bought two radio-controlled toy speed boats to chase the ducks on the water to make them fly, but it only worked twice – the ducks soon got used to them.

I know of a farmer who rents a big farm on an estate. There is a large lake next to his buildings and quite a lot of duck are reared there for the shoot. No matter how quiet and devious they are, the duck always seem to know when the Range Rovers start arriving so the ducks start walking into the nearby cattle sheds; there would be up to 500 there on occasion. So the guns are quietly spaced out and all is ready and the trouble is there is not a duck to be seen. The keeper comes on the farmer's yard and asks the farmer if he's seen any ducks this morning and the farmer says that there were plenty on the lake half an hour ago. But as he doesn't much like the keeper, he makes no mention of all the ducks in his cattle sheds. So the 4x4's drive on, duckless, and the ducks walk back to the water.

I was once invited to go on a very grand shoot where you had a loader assigned to you. Most of the 'guns' had two shotguns so the loader could always pass them a loaded gun. We started on the ducks, there was a big lake nearby, and I shot as many as I could. Then all the ducks that hadn't been shot disappeared into the distance and the man doing my loading said we wait now and they will start coming back. And they did, some were really high, so high they were out of range, then there were some that were lower and the loader made to pass me my gun. I declined it and said that I didn't believe anything should be shot at twice. I didn't mind shooting at the ducks the first time but believed they were entitled to some peace when they came back. I am sure this was reported back. Most of the other guns were good shots and proceeded to shoot high birds and low birds. I wasn't invited again but I don't ever regret what I said; if you have principals you should not be afraid to stand up for them.

I can remember that I once bought 24-day-old Mallard ducklings and kept them as pets. As soon as they were old enough I put them on our pond. The milking parlour was surely 200 yards from the pond and the route between the two was not straightforward, but twice a day, at the end of milking, they would march in single file, like 25 soldiers, to visit the parlour. When they got there they would search for any cake that the cows had dropped and eat it. When it was all gone, they would march back. I loved to see them about.

They were safe on the pond because there is a small island there. In the following spring the females started building nests in nearby hedgerows and the drakes would stand guard. I never bought any more. If they couldn't live a natural life I didn't want to know. The fox killed the lot in one night. If the fox had killed one for a meal I could understand it but I could never understand this wanton killing. That's why foxes are usually so unpopular in rural areas. I never had much sympathy for foxes, over the years they have killed lots of my poultry and lambs. But a bit like the ducks being shot at twice, I always thought that if a fox made it back to a hole, it shouldn't be dug out and despatched. It had won the day and was deserving of another. Another thing I have never understood: there is no shortage of hunt saboteurs and anti-hunting with dogs But you never hear of people, conservationists or wildlife trusts criticising hare coursers.

21 May 2022

My eldest grandson, who lives up the yard in a mobile home, is a prolific online shopper. The van drivers haven't worked out where he lives so all his parcels get dropped off here. I read somewhere that his generation blames my generation for global warming. There were four vans here this afternoon. One of the vans was a Royal Mail van and he could have bought the lot. In fact you could have easily put the four parcels in a wheelbarrow and still have had room for more. When I was his age our parcels were delivered by the postman who had a sort of carrier on the front of his bike. There's nothing as green as that going on these days!

***

Mind over matter! There used to be a retired man who came to the pub once a week. He had worked all his life for the BBC and he was always interesting company. We used to talk endlessly about Welsh rugby. I remember saying to him that I was going to see Wales play Ireland in Dublin in two weeks' time and in a lot of ways I wasn't looking forward to it. Naturally he wanted to know why I and so I told him. We had gone to Dublin two years previously and I had suffered terrible sea sickness. The second class area was packed with noisy rugby fans, the floors were awash with spilled beer and vomit and I was terribly sick. I was ok if it was on deck but it was so cold. I spent all night there, there were no seats because they were all taken and when we were finally let loose at 8am I wasn't in a very good shape.

My friend when he heard this story said, 'I can fix that for you.' We arranged to meet the next week on the Wednesday, and he brought with him a white envelope. He tipped the contents onto the table and there were lots of tablets all wrapped separately in white paper, a bit like the police find when they do a drugs bust. He said, 'All these tablets have a time and date written on them, you must start in the morning by taking half a tablet when you get up and another half when you go to bed. On Friday when you get up take a whole one and another whole one when you get on the ferry.' 'What about coming back?' I asked. 'Keep yourself topped up with tablets all day on Saturday and again on Sunday and you should be OK. Meet me here in a week's time to tell me how you got on.' I did everything as he suggested, to the letter, and I was fine, both there and back.

I met him on the Wednesday night as arranged and told him I hadn't had any sea sickness. 'What were those tablets?' 'They were junior disprin, they have nothing to do with sea sickness, that was all in your mind.' And so there is another of life's lessons.

***

I may as well tell you the rest of the story. The second class accommodation was terrible on the late night ferry. It was packed – you'd never be allowed to move animals like that. But we had a plan. We stopped on shore as long as we could, but when the pubs closed we boarded the ferry. That was the only place where they were still serving so by the time it sailed, we had had several pints and some fish and chips. We waited until the ferry had left the harbour and then we went on deck. We climbed over the rail and went hand over hand along the side of the ship until we could get back over the rail. By then we were in first class. In there, there were fewer people, lots of empty comfortable armchairs and altogether a better experience. I don't think of it very often but it was probably the stupidest thing I have ever done. We must have gone twenty yards outside that ship, and we waited until we were out of the harbour and in rougher seas. By the time the ship had stopped and turned around we would have had hypothermia. One of my nine lives went that night. Doesn't bear thinking about.

28 May 2022

I once went to a dinner in the north of England. It was a Young Farmers dinner, a big occasion, as far as I remember it was their 100th anniversary. Apparently, it was a tradition that their youngest member should say grace. I'll always remember, this little fair haired boy came up to the front, I would guess he was about ten, and this is what he said, 'We that are sinners, give thanks for our dinners.' I remember thinking then, what good training there was at young farmers. Youngsters might not be called upon to say grace to lots of people very often but there's a fair chance when they are older they will have to make speeches or give interviews and can take that confidence with them.

***

There is a debate on at home on the cost of food and as a consequence of that, food waste and 'best before dates'. Some time ago a good friend called by on his way to visit a supermarket. He said he was going there to buy a frozen oven-ready goose and so I asked him to get me one. There was only one trouble, my wife doesn't like eating goose so when mine arrived it went into the chest freezer. There it stayed. About twice a year I remembered it and used to say, 'Don't forget, we still have that goose to eat.' But I usually got fobbed off with an excuse as to why the goose would stay in the freezer. One day I said to my daughter that if she were to invite us to Sunday dinner, I would supply an oven-ready goose for the occasion. She agreed right away and after some difficulty we found the goose where it was languishing at the very bottom of the chest freezer. And very good it was too. When we were eating it my daughter said, 'Do you know how long it was past its best before date? Four years!' It's two weeks now since we ate the goose, no one has been ill, not even the dog Gomer and George the robin, who picked over the bones. The best before date is merely a suggestion.

4 June 2022

A gang of us some time ago decided to fly to Ireland to watch the rugby. It was quicker and less physically demanding than the ferry but now we went on Thursdays lest the effects of jet lag should spoil our weekend. Then I had a good idea. In Dublin we only met other Welsh supporters but if we moved out of Dublin we would meet Irishmen. Completely at random we chose a town on the main road to Belfast about half an hour from Dublin. The hotel had been closed since the autumn and I can remember it was cold and damp and that lorries thundered past all night long. I was sharing a double bed with my best friend and we were so cold that we slept with most of our clothes on and cwtched up to try to keep warm.

Anyway we arrived at this hotel late on the Thursday afternoon, settled in and then went outside to see where we were. Opposite us was a pub and that seemed a good place to start. It was indeed a good place to start because it was the headquarters of the local rugby club. They had never had Welsh supporters staying in their town before so we were a bit of a novelty and they made a fuss of us. I don't think any of us were allowed to buy a drink all night.

The local butcher asked me what we planned to do on the Friday and I said we would probably go into Dublin. 'Sure, you will need my Land Rover. If you call at my shop after you have had your breakfast I will have it ready for you.' And he did, it was full of petrol and we had the use of it all weekend. True it was six months out of tax but never mind. They were lively company in the pub but it soon became obvious to me that some of them weren't speaking to one another, they were circling like warring dogs with their hackles raised. I was determined to get to the bottom of it. If was quite easy because each person involved was keen to tell me their side of the story.

Our friend the butcher was the main player. Turns out he also has a farm and the summer before he had some hay cut. His thinking was that if it was turned twice on the Saturday, it would bale on the Sunday. Trouble was that Saturday was a busy day in his shop. The forecast wasn't brilliant so he asked a contractor if he would turn his hay on the Saturday. The contractor, who was also in the pub, hadn't been to the butcher's farm before, lost his way and proceeded to turn a neighbour's hay. The neighbour who was also there, was just going to turn his hay but sees someone else doing it, let's him get on with it and stays in his house all day. It all gets a bit complicated now: the butcher gets home expecting to see his hay all turned and it wasn't. The contractor sends a bill for his day's work but the neighbour refuses to pay him because he never asked him to do this work. So the butcher isn't talking to the contractor, the contractor isn't talking to the neighbour, the neighbour isn't talking to the butcher, you get the picture I'm sure. But I had them all talking by the end of the evening.

The first time we went there one of our party was a man who had just left the armed forces after about 15 years. He liked to plan all that we did, and he used a 24 hour clock to do it. We took no notice of him and he had his work cut out with us but we were as nothing compared to the Irish. We went across to the pub on Sunday morning and one of the Irishmen asked him about our travel arrangements to get back home. 'We will get some taxis at 1300 hours to take us to the airport,' our man said. 'Sure there's no need for taxis, we'll take you to the airport and 2.30 will allow you plenty of time.' And so they did, a fleet of local cars took us to the airport. They parked where they shouldn't have parked, they dropped us off where they shouldn't. They never paid a penny for parking. And we had to run for the plane. Sure, it didn't matter, I'm at home now aren't I?

11 June 2022

I'm watching the red kites scouring our valley. There's a river there and several water courses and I have always assumed that they were after waterbirds or their young. I don't know where the kites live but there are several big woods close at hand and the kites are such accomplished fliers that these big woods are only a kite's wing beat away.

But this year there is a big difference. In the foreground, at the top of a tree, and not there last year, is a carrion crow's nest. The kites normal flight path takes it right over this nest and the two carrion crows fly out each time to do battle. Some fierce fights take place. As far as I can make out the adversaries are trying to drive each other to the ground. I've not seen this happen yet but I have seen them drop to 2-3 feet above ground. What would happen if either were to be successful I dread to think.

If I lower my gaze just a little bit I can see our pond. At this time of year it is taken over by Canada geese. A week ago, five goslings appeared but now there are only two. All day long the pond is visited by kites and carrion crows and I am assuming that this is where the three missing goslings are gone. I know that there are plenty of Canada geese about and I know that this is what carrion crows and kites do, but the loss of these three makes me a bit sad, for a while. And then if I go into the kitchen, George the robin is always there. I sometimes think that he spends more time in our kitchen than he does outside. If my wife is not about at midday he comes down to watch the news with me. My wife thinks it's her robin; little does she know.

***

Hasn't it been a wonderful year for the bluebells. I've seen bluebells where I haven't seen them before. I've seen spectacular carpets of them in woodland. Of course they were there all the time, what has brought them out in such profusion this year, I have no idea.

***

I can hear some carrion crows outside the back door so I go to see what they are doing. Seems some sparrows have just fledged in the creeper and the crows are having a bit of a clear out. You are supposed to turn a blind eye to this sort of predation but I quite like sparrows so I shoo the crows off. I notice that George is keeping his head well down.

25 June 2022

We've just had Gomer clipped. Now we can all see how fat he is. He looks a bit like a biscuit barrel on four legs. Everyone who calls here laughs at him and so he spends most of his time under tables thinking he is out of sight. He doesn't just have humans laughing at him, he also has George the robin laughing as well. George is getting far too cheeky for my liking, he spends a lot of time in our living room watching TV. We have Robin poo on our TV screen. Not a lot of people can say that.
Naturally this is my fault.

Also by Roger Evans

A Farmer's Lot
A View from the Tractor
Pull the Other One!
How Now?
Fifty Bales of Hay

ebook only
Over the Farmer's Gate

Further reading from
Merlin Unwin Books

Don't Worry He Doesn't Bite! Liam Mulvin
A Job for all Seasons Phyllida Barstow
My Animals (and Other Family) Phyllida Barstow
Full English Edward Miller
Maynard, Adventures of a Bacon Curer Maynard Davies
Maynard, Secrets of a Bacon Curer Maynard Davies

For full details of these books
www.merlinunwin.co.uk